Tim Steer toured with Meat Loaf, Diana Ross, Cheap Trick, The Cars, the Small Faces and Thin Lizzy as a sound engineer, and managed Pink Floyd's sound and lighting system after the release of *The Wall*. At the time it was one of the largest systems in the world. He then embarked on a new career, qualifying as a Chartered Accountant with Ernst & Young before becoming a highly rated investment analyst with HSBC and then Merrill Lynch. In 2000 he joined fund managers New Star and subsequently Artemis, and was one of the top-ranked fund managers in the UK, being rated AAA by Citywire. He has written regularly for the *Sunday Times* and *Sunday Telegraph* and featured in the 2018 Channel 4 Dispatches documentary on the collapse of Carillion.

Praise for *The Signs Were

'Helpful and enjoyably read

'Tim Steer shines a light on the murkiest corners of corporate accounting – and what he discovers is horrendous and hilarious in equal measure. The secrets of the balance sheet are exposed, making this a must-read for investors big or small.' William Lewis, CEO Dow Jones and Publisher of the *Wall Street Journal*

'The best book I have ever read about accounting ... Buy this book. It's a worthwhile investment.' Ben Wright, *Daily Telegraph*

'Topical and informative, this book is a worthy successor to Terry Smith's *Accounting for Growth* – and about time too.' Oliver Shah, Business Editor, *Sunday Times*

'For every credit there's a debit – it's where you put them is the problem. Tim Steer's incisive eye and common-sense approach unfortunately is not common in the market.' Andy Brough, Head of Pan-European Small Companies, Schroders

'Essential reading for any financial journalist hoping to spot the next Carillion, iSoft or Autonomy.' Richard Fletcher, Business Editor, *The Times*

THE SIGNS WERE THERE

THE CLUES FOR INVESTORS THAT
A COMPANY IS HEADING FOR A FALL

TIM STEER

P

PROFILE BOOKS

This revised edition published in 2019

First published in Great Britain in 2018 by
Profile Books Ltd
29 Cloth Fair
London EC1A 7JQ

www.profilebooks.com

Designed and typeset by Sue Lamble

Printed and bound in Great Britain by
Clays Ltd, Elcograf S.p.A.

A CIP catalogue record for this book is available from the
British Library.

ISBN 978 1 78816 081 0
eISBN 978 178283 462 5

For Andrea and Thomas

Contents

Acknowledgements

This book is written for the many who invest on their own account or for others, but it celebrates the few who recognise the significance and importance of a company's financial statements. Of all the people I know, those who count among the few are listed below and include those who have been an inspiration to me. All have enquiring minds and have sought answers to difficult questions. Many have done the right thing in difficult circumstances – and in some cases at a cost to themselves. On behalf of all investors I would like to thank them for their vigilance.

Adrian Frost	Barney Randle	David Toms
Adrian Gosden	Ben Martin	Derek Stuart
Alan Brierley	Ben Wright	Emma Mercer
Alan Miller	Bruce Davidson	Eric Tracey
Alistair Currie	Charles Lambert	Euan Lovett-Turner
Alistair Osborne	Chris Bamberry	Frank Field
Andrew Jackson	Daniel Grote	Frank Manduca
Andy Bamford	Daud Khan	Gavin James
Andy Brough	David Bamber	Gavin Oram
Angus Cockburn	David Hellier	George Godber
Ashton Bradbury	David McCann	George Luckcraft

Gerald Khoo

Harald Hendrikse

Harry Nimmo

Henry Dixon

Howard Seymour

Howard Shilit

Iain Dey

Jacob de Tusch-Lec

James Nadin

James Quinn

Joe Brent

John Collingridge

John Waples

Jon Lewis

Katharine Wynne

Kean Marden

Keith Cochrane

Kevin Ashton

Leo Quinn

Louise Armitstead

Mal Patel

Margaret Young

Mark Tyndall

Martin Green

Martin Hughes

Mary Hardy

Matthew Earl

Matthew Groves

Max Dolding

Michael Donnelly

Mike Geering

Mike Sheen

Mike Unsworth

Miles Costello

Mohamed Haman

Natalie Kenway

Natasha Landell-Mills

Neil Blackley

Neil Hermon

Neil Roberts

Nigel Ridge

Nigel Thomas

Oliver Shah

Paul Hogg

Paul Morland

Peter Davies

Peter Dickinson

Peter Smedley

Phil Bentley

Phil Oakley

Quintin Price

Richard Dale

Richard Findlater

Richard Fletcher

Richard King

Richard Leonard

Richard Plackett

Roger Hardman

Roger Phillips

Rosemary Banyard

Rupert Soames

Ruth Keattch

Simon Cawkwell

Sir David Tweedie

Stephen Liechti

Stephen Rawlinson

Stephen Yiu

Terry Smith

Tim Good

Wes McCoy

Will Lewis

William Tamworth

Introduction

THE HIGH CLIFF DIVERS OF ACAPULCO

Company share price disasters are like the plunges made by the famous high cliff divers of Acapulco. This is because the 135-feet dives that these brave men make from the cliffs of La Quebrada into the shallow waters below resemble what the share prices of companies do when they go spectacularly wrong. However, among the high cliff divers of Acapulco, there has never been a casualty, whereas a precipitous drop – or even a more drawn out extended swallow dive – in a company's share price may well result in it going bust, with shareholders, employees, suppliers, bankers, auditors and now, increasingly, even regulators caught by the shock waves. Some companies do of course recover, often with new management at the helm, but even then the fall-out for shareholders and other stakeholders following the share price collapse can be severe.

For all the companies featured in this book, the dives in the share prices and the company disasters that resulted in bankruptcy could have been predicted by little more than a browse through the annual reports or prospectuses if you knew where to look. But it seems that many of the great and the good in the world of investing do not bother to look at these important documents, and blame the auditors – and increasingly the regulators – when things go wrong. But the warning signs are regularly there, in the form of accounting shenanigans or other clear signs in the annual report that a business is changing direction for the worse, or that excellent results are being reported only because of one-off and non-recurring items. Often these red flags are either not seen or are ignored by investors and other stakeholders.

The collapse in January 2018 of Carillion, which had received enormous amounts of public money as one of the UK government's favourite construction and support services companies, is just one in a long line of corporate disasters where even a cursory look at the balance sheet by anyone with a smattering of financial training would have evoked a feeling of déjà vu and the realisation that the company was heading for a fall. Of course, not all share price disasters can be predicted by reading the annual report of a company, but it is a start and, with a little bit of knowledge, issues can be identified and a potential loss-making decision avoided. This book is aimed at helping investors see the signs that there may be trouble ahead.

When looking at annual reports, always consider the Iceberg Principle. An annual report should be seen as an iceberg in terms of the information it contains. It cannot tell you all you need to know about a company, but if there is something in it that makes you feel uneasy, there may well be other even more uncomfortable things lying below the metaphorical water line. And that is often reason enough to sell the shares if you have a holding in the company, or to avoid it if you have not.

This book contains twenty-seven stories about companies that suffered dramatic falls in their share prices and one well-known investment fund. Some of the companies survived the fall, some did not. But in the cases of twenty-three of these companies there were clear signs in their annual reports that all was not well, and in the initial public offering (IPO) prospectuses of the other four companies, there were items that should have raised a quizzical eyebrow or two among potential investors. Although around half of the companies featured in this book got to grips with their problems and survived, thanks to the efforts and strategy of new management, the others did not.

The share price disasters suffered by the twenty-seven companies in this book are presented in groups, as there are common themes. History repeats itself, it would seem – and I should make the point that the sins that companies commit are rarely confined to just one theme.

Carillion, for example, had the stamp of another construction and support services company called Amey, which was also one of the UK government's favourite private finance initiative (PFI) contractors in its day. As shown in their annual reports, both companies experienced a very sharp deterioration in the quality of their current assets, leading up to a precipitous decline in their share prices. Both companies had rising debt, so converting current assets into cash was important. But the cash conversion did not come through for either of them – which should have come as no surprise to those who had inspected their annual reports.

The cash did not come through at the outsourcing company Capita either. With a tendency to emphasise so called 'underlying profits' to investors at results presentations rather than the lower profits that were actually reported, Capita's annual reports also showed that current asset quality was declining at a fast rate with a large increase in accrued income in particular. No surprises then that new management were quick to refinance the company as the accrued income was, well, not incoming at all.

The UK's only remaining luxury car maker Aston Martin Lagonda (AML) came to the market in 2018 and priced its shares at £19. The shares have free-wheeled downhill since then perhaps because by the look of the trade receivable balance included in current assets, the distribution channel to the dealers looked well-stuffed. Current asset quality falls the longer the dealers take to pay and this was obvious from the AML prospectus. No wonder the shares of AML have fallen badly since the flotation.

Northern Rock, the UK's biggest mortgage lender at the time of its collapse, and Cattles, a doorstep lender to the less well off, had similarities too. Whilst Northern Rock's financing weaknesses were exposed by the financial crisis of 2007–8, both companies were far too optimistic as to the great British public's intentions to pay off their debts. This was clear from the annual reports published by both of them before their dramatic demises. With both, lending to customers rose aggressively but their bad debt provision did not. Even the chairmen's statements used the same language to underscore the importance they attached to 'growth', 'credit quality' and 'efficiency' – unfortunately, they both forgot that anyone can lend money, it is getting it back that is the difficult bit.

One of the UK's largest software companies, Autonomy, which was acquired by Hewlett-Packard in 2011, had the whiff of iSoft about it in the way it recognised revenue from the sale of software. The lessons of iSoft, the company at the heart of one of the world's largest failed IT projects to join up the UK's National Health Service digitally, were seemingly ignored by Hewlett-Packard and its legion of advisers.

Large accruals of income are warning signs that there may be trouble ahead. Accruals of income are after all only estimates and therefore dependent sometimes on over optimistic and enthusiastic management. I am being kind here of course. There was certainly optimism and enthusiasm by management which resulted in trouble for iSoft, Cedar Group, Utilitywise, Redcentric and the renowned Australian law firm Slater and Gordon, which foolishly acquired Quindell's personal injury business for cash in 2015. All these companies had accruals of income in spades. Slater and Gordon paid £637 million for a business that had as its main asset an accrual of income that amounted to 40% of the year's sales. They may wish now that they had not gone anywhere near Quindell as the value of Slater and Gordon shares have collapsed to virtually nothing, having been valued at over A$2 billion at one point. You see, all that accrued income never translated into cash.

The method employed by energy broker Utilitywise to recognise the revenues due from its energy suppliers depended on valuing an expected stream of commissions using a discount rate that reflected the risk that these may not be paid. To some people's shock, Utilitywise suddenly reduced this discount rate by two-thirds with the obvious result that revenues and profits were dramatically increased. This significant change was tucked away in the annual report but just like the iceberg tip above the waterline it was a warning sign to steer clear. There was just too much flexibility in how Utilitywise made up its accounts.

Cedar Group's shares tumbled like timber in the middle of a failed rights issue when it became obvious that the company was waiting on average nine months for its cash from the sale of software. In all probability the truth was that Cedar Group's clients did not think that they owed the company that money. It was pretty much the same sorry story years later at another software company called iSoft, where aggressive revenue recognition policies allowed sales to be significantly overstated. But a massive accrual of income of £50 million in the 2004 iSoft Annual Report was a warning sign that many missed. It was also a large accrued income balance and window dressing generally that should have been a red light for investors in IT company Redcentric in 2016. A forensic review by Deloitte and Nabarro found assets had been overstated by £15.8 million and debt understated by £12.5 million. Surprising really because Redcentric, iSoft and Cedar Group were doppelgängers. Only some learn from past mistakes it seems.

Run a mile if you see related party transactions. UK investors got caught up in two small companies called Healthcare Locums and Erinaceous where the directors played happy families. Of course, doing business with friends and family was not the reason the share prices of these two companies collapsed but it should have been enough for investors to raise an eyebrow and put on their running shoes.

In the world of blue collar outsourcing, Mitie had parallels with failed Connaught but, thanks to the arrival of new management, the similarities were short-lived – although only after they had had to significantly restate previous years' numbers. There were quite a few accounting shenanigans at Mitie and Connaught. Both of these outsourcing companies capitalised significant start-up costs incurred in organising new contracts which allowed profits to be overstated.

NCC, a cyber security company that really ought to have been doing rather well, also capitalised significant items that allowed profits to keep moving ahead – until they confessed that the development and software costs they had accounted for as assets rather than expenses were no longer recoverable at all. But this was not before they had raised cash for an acquisition by issuing shares at a price that reflected that all the development and software costs were going to be recovered.

Goodwill for Mitie and Carillion turned to badwill. It was not so blatantly badwill at Carillion but at Mitie it was, as the company continued to overvalue it as an asset even though the trading of a recently acquired healthcare company included in goodwill was deteriorating fast and significant losses were being reported. It said so in the 2016 Mitie Annual Report, so how could they justify a recoverable amount of £145 million for this business? The answer was they could not and they soon sold this business ... for just £2!

Tribal Group is now an educational software company and is doing well, but previously it had been a mish-mash and it suffered two share price dives. Too many acquisitions meant it lacked focus and frankly there were just too many tribes in the group to give coherence in the jungle of local government. And then it started accruing rather large amounts of income on certain contracts that well ... went wrong.

Acquisitive companies often do not add shareholder value. Just ask all those investors who supported the acquisition of Matthew Clark, a doyen of the UK drinks sector, by Bargain Booze owner and new kid on the block, Conviviality. They must have been under the influence. The accounts clearly showed that Conviviality was feeling the effects of 'acquisitionitis' as it had to have two bites of the cherry(ade) as they reappraised and reduced the fair value of assets acquired at Matthew Clark some 22 months after buying it. That told us all we needed to know about the financial nous at Conviviality and, with that, its ability to manage large acquisitions and indeed its own business. It should have come as no surprise that Conviviality failed to account for tax and made mistakes in its forecasting.

Guardian IT, once the UK's leading disaster recovery company, had its own disaster when it purchased leading rival Safetynet. The acquisition was no safety net for Guardian IT, though, as expectations at Safetynet were not met. Guardian IT, once a tech boom star, was gobbled up at a fraction of its former share price by SunGard Data Systems of the US. But it was clear from earlier annual reports that Guardian IT was not growing its core business but relying on acquisitions for growth.

It was obvious too that Slater and Gordon's acquisition of Quindell's personal injury business and Hewlett-Packard's acquisition of Autonomy were bound to destroy shareholder value because neither of the acquirees' accounts stacked up – in both cases there was just too much subjectivity in revenue recognition. Neither Slater and Gordon nor Hewlett-Packard, it appeared, did the required level of due diligence expected of management.

Arthur Andersen moved from the limelight into the spotlight when Enron went bust. Enron had paid Arthur Andersen $27 million for non-audit services and $25 million for audit services which made this energy trading company one of its biggest clients. Arthur Andersen even felt that fees could top $100 million in total if things went their way. There were clear conflicts of interests here and when non-audit services reach a material level it is a warning sign that the numbers in the accounts may be more fiction than fact. That was the case at Findel, a UK discount retailer whose share price collapsed.

As a famous investment saying goes, a trend can be your friend. Analysing a series of numbers from one year to another would have been a useful exercise for investors in Toshiba. Normally balance sheet items like debtors and creditors move roughly in tandem with a company's activity levels. When this trend is broken, further investigation is required. Sinking sales, a declining depreciation charge, soaring stock levels and plummeting profits between 2007 and 2013 could have been easily spotted at Toshiba. But this tawdry tale masked an even worse picture when profits were found to be overstated by some 40% following an enquiry by the Tokyo regulator. Management fell on their samurai swords.

Pets at Home, a chain of large petshops, finally floated its shares on the London Stock Exchange in 2014. The trend in margins in the preceding period indicated they had already peaked as the company and clever private equity holders benefited hugely from pooch loving consumers switching their preference from low margin wet food in tins to higher margin dry food, leaving little upside left for the new investors.

At AO World, an internet retailer of washing machines and other white goods, a spike in spending on advertising with search engines – which was clearly shown in the company's helpful IPO documents – indicated that there was a new cost paradigm in play and previous profits were going to be difficult to replicate. That the trend of pedestrian growth in advertising with search engines like Google was over for this online retailer was either not seen by some investors, or just ignored. AO World has yet to report a profit since it floated – partly because of increased marketing expenditure – but curiously it did in the year before it listed its shares on the stock exchange, when spending on marketing was lower and directors offloaded shares to some established investors.

A recent company disaster was Interserve. There were no obvious signs of a decline in the quality of current assets here, it was just a rubbish business with a trend of tiny margins and a habit of having no cash generation. Interserve could therefore ill-afford a large contract going wrong, which it did and a rubbish contract at that.

Sports Direct was another disastrous IPO. The shares dived like a swallow for 20 months after flotation, losing nearly 90% of their value. Of course that could have been because England's finest footballers failed to qualify for the 2008 UEFA European Championship and Sports Direct had forecast good sales of white shirts bearing the three lions, but a glance at the IPO prospectus showed an unusual adjustment to inventories in the year before the flotation of the company that was worthy of a question or two.

It is always difficult to detect fraud from a company's annual report. Just ask Luke Johnson and most of his board who even missed it right in front of their noses. But the level of inventory at Patisserie Holdings (the owner of cake shop Patisserie Valerie) indicated that the cakes there may have been 80 days old before being consumed if the company's accounts were to be believed.

So red flags everywhere. It is often the use of optimistic estimates, coupled with a liberal interpretation of certain accounting standards, that are the problem. The trouble with the UK's current accounting standards is that they are too principles-based and allow leeway in the manner they are interpreted and applied. US accounting standards, by contrast, are far more rigid and prescriptive. IFRS 15 – Revenue from Contracts with Customers, a new accounting standard jointly agreed by the IASB (International Accounting Standards Board) and FASB (Financial Accounting Standards Board in the US), which came into force in January 2018, should put an end to the early recognition of revenues in a company's accounts. It has taken sixteen years to create. Had it been around earlier, many of the recent accounting shenanigans we have seen in IT and support services companies in particular may not have occurred.

In the meantime, it is worth remembering one thing: in any annual report, cash is fact (except in the case of outright fraud, as at the Italian dairy firm Parmalat, where $4.5 billion of cash was reported but did not exist) and everything else is a matter of opinion – or an estimate. Annual reports should be read from the back to the front, with scepticism and the understanding that auditors have limits on their investigative skills and are working under tight budgets. They often have to rely on management assurances for their information and they will not get it right all the time. Watchdogs, not bloodhounds, come to mind.

Perhaps investors should be forgiven for getting the odd stock pick wrong by failing to spot the signs in the annual reports of companies that are included in their portfolios. But it is inexcusable to make a series of blunders in determining the constituents of a portfolio as was the case with the Woodford Equity Income Fund (WEIF). A perusal of the helpful WEIF monthly fact sheets published on the Woodford Investment Management (WIM) web site showed that numerous tried and tested rules were disregarded that led to a once famous fund manager having to suspend dealings in his fund. If Neil Woodford had been a wine grower, then in the past he would have been responsible for producing some of the world's finest vintages, instead at his new venture he produced muddy water.

The concluding chapter of this book looks at what is wrong with the way the system – in terms of auditing, regulation, and so on – currently works and makes some suggestions as to how things may be changed for the better. All that apart, the overriding hope and aim of this book is to help investors to avoid the kinds of foreseeable disasters that its chapters examine.

Picking stock market winners consistently is very difficult – which is why even the very best professional investors rarely stay at the top of their game for ever. But avoiding stock market disasters – which is probably more important than picking winners – through the simple analysis of annual reports and the application of the Iceberg Principle can be done regardless of what themes and trends are playing out in financial markets. In this respect, the lessons in this book will help investors to be on top of their game all of the time.

PART 1

Abracadabra

HOW PROFITS CAN BE MAXIMISED BY TURNING COSTS INTO ASSETS

One way to make costs disappear is to change them into something different by calling them assets. That way the costs are removed from the income statement to the balance sheet, profits keep moving ahead, expectations are met, management keep their well-paid jobs and share prices stay up. This is allowed under International Accounting Standard (IAS) 38 – Intangible Assets, which states that development costs incurred by a company must be accounted for in this way as long as certain criteria are met. These criteria are:

- The costs are part of a project that is technically feasible and will be available for use or sale.
- There is the intention to complete the project – i.e. create the intangible asset.

- It can be demonstrated that the intangible asset will produce future economic benefits – i.e. that there is a market or economic use to the company for the product of the development expenditure.
- The company has adequate resources available to complete the development.
- The costs of the intangible can be reliably measured.

Once development costs have been capitalised (that is, counted as an asset rather than an expense), they are amortised (that is, the costs are gradually written off) over their useful life, starting from the point the asset is available for use. The trouble with cyber security specialists NCC, one of the two companies that feature in this section, was that the amortisation of internally generated software took place very slowly and development costs were not amortised at all. This kept profits up until, every now and then, these capitalised costs were written off through the income statement – which indicated that they probably should not have been capitalised in the first place.

Connaught, the failed public sector support services company that also features in this chapter, capitalised large amounts of staff costs it attributed to building a new software system. There is nothing wrong with this, but the amount being capitalised should have prompted suspicions. Connaught also capitalised large costs that had been incurred ahead of starting certain contracts. These costs were known as mobilisation costs and another International Accounting Standard, IAS 11 – Construction Contracts, allowed them to be capitalised and written off over the term of the contract. However, again, it was the size of these costs at Connaught that should have raised concerns, especially as some of its competitors did not capitalise such costs but wrote them off.

The overriding lesson of intangibles included in a company's annual report is that they cannot be precisely assessed or defined. Because of this, they offer great scope for companies to massage their profits (up or down) and so are always worth looking at with care in a company's annual report.

Connaught

NAUGHT FOR SHAREHOLDERS

Between 2004 and 2009 Connaught reported 48% compound growth in profits and was a stock market darling, but in 2010 it collapsed into administration. Shareholders got nothing. The company was founded in 1982 as a concrete repair specialist and by the 1990s had diversified into becoming an outsourcer for social housing services, fixing windows, doors and boilers for local authorities and housing associations. A management buyout in 1996 was predictably followed in 1998 by a float on the Alternative Investment Market (AIM), the London Stock Exchange's more lightly regulated stock market for less viable companies. By 2004 Connaught had revenues of around £300 million and negligible net debt, and was busy acquiring related businesses. A listing on the main market of the London Stock Exchange (LSE) took place in 2006, and in 2007 Connaught became a constituent of the important FTSE 250. The admission of the shares to the main market allowed Connaught to raise money through share issues, extend its range of activities and make even more acquisitions, such as environmental services companies National Britannia for

over £90 million in 2007 and Fountains for £13 million in 2009. Nothing could stop this dynamic company, it seemed.

But in January 2010, Mark Davies, the chief executive of Connaught since 2005, who armed with his MBA from INSEAD had previously been managing director at Chubb in the UK, suddenly departed – although not before he had sold £5.5 million of shares. Things were going so well at Connaught, everyone thought. Why had he left and sold shares? In spite of a reassuring statement from the company saying that 'the board believes the business continues to perform well and the outlook for the group remains robust', the shares were on their way to naught. A letter from management to staff, sent in April 2010, blamed the ensuing

Connaught shares on their way to naught

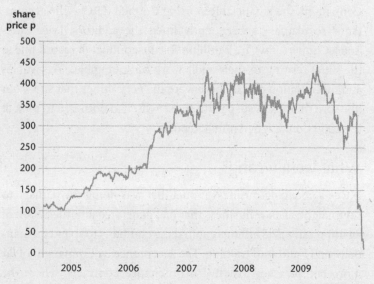

Source: Datastream

dramatic fall in the share price on hedge funds shorting the shares and a 'fundamentally flawed and very mediocre analyst's note which simply repeated unfounded rumours and nonsense from the past, whilst getting the numbers wrong at the same time', which was, they said, 'a masterful feat of incompetence.'

Management should have blamed no one but themselves for Connaught's woes. It was their failure to anticipate and cope with large changes in the demands from new clients that meant unexpected costs were incurred. And it was management that hid these costs in the balance sheet in order not to disturb important profit expectations and, of course, the share price. In the end, cash flow was so poor and the company's debt had risen to such levels that its banking covenants were broken – and not even a new chairman, city grandee Sir Roy Gardner of Manchester United, Centrica and Compass Group fame, could rescue it. Following the collapse of Connaught, the Financial Reporting Council (FRC) – the accountants' regulator – subsequently fined the auditors, PricewaterhouseCoopers (PwC), £5 million for misconduct (a record fine at the time) relating to their audit work on intangibles, receivables and mobilisation costs. These were the very things that stuck out like sore thumbs as suspect to those who had bothered to look at the 2009 Connaught Annual Report.

What went wrong?

It was a changing business model that was doing the damage to Connaught, as new business that had generated an order book of an impressive £2.8 billion required the company to spend substantially on IT and staff training. The acceptance by Connaught of far more complex and reactive maintenance contracts, where the customer could call on the company to fix boilers, doors and so on at short notice, required a whole new infrastructure. Connaught's customers, many of whom were local authorities, became more and more demanding it seemed, while contracts became bigger and more complicated. Increased investment was required. These new investments hit cash flow hard and debt rose, and in order to prevent these costs from disturbing the growth in profits expected by investors, Connaught capitalised them and described them as assets in the balance sheet.

Tipping point and warning signs

Plastered on the cover of the 2009 Connaught Annual Report were the words 'Sustainable Business, Consistently Delivering' – comforting words for those creditors, customers, investors and employees who took them at face value. In fact, nothing could have been further from the truth: the small print of that report revealed that the company was keeping operating costs away from the important income statement and so was overstating its profits. The balance sheet told the real story, not the income statement. There were two main hiding places for certain costs in the 2009 Connaught Annual Report: Note 15 – Trade and other receivables and Note 11 – Intangible assets.

In **Note 15 – Trade and other receivables** (see next page), there were large amounts recoverable on contracts, which apparently reflected 'accounts which are recoverable over the period of the contracts to which they relate'. This was odd, giving the impression that this receivable would take quite a while to recover, if indeed it was recoverable at all. Discussions with the company's management indicated that these were mobilisation costs or set-up

Note 15: Trade and other receivables, an extract, £m

2009	Total	Not yet due	Past due months 1–3	Impaired months 3–6	Impaired months 6+
Trade receivables	49.8	**31.8**	14.1	1.4	2.5
Amounts recoverable on contracts	105.0	**101.0**	2.7	0.5	0.8
	154.8	132.8	16.8	1.9	3.3

The ageing profile for trade receivables includes trade receivables and retentions owed by customers, net of bad debt provisions amounting to £1.6m *(2008 £1.8m)*. The movement of bad debt provisions during the year was not material for purposes of further disclosure.

Included in the amounts receivable on contracts within the ageing profile is both amounts receivable held under current and non-current assets respectively. Other receivables are excluded from the above analysis and have been treated as not yet due £2.9m *(2008 £3.4m)*.

Amounts recoverable on contracts represent the estimated amounts which have been earned or which valuation, under the terms of the respective contracts, have not yet been agreed with the customers. These amounts have been included at their estimated recoverable values. Included within accounts not yet due is **£27.8m** *(2008 £12.6m)* which reflects accounts which are recoverable over the period of the contracts to which they relate. Accounts which are over six months overdue and are still to be agreed by the customers are prudently valued at their estimated written-down recoverable value.

Source: 2009 Connaught Annual Report

Capitalisation of mobilisation costs

costs incurred on the initiation of new contracts. But the amounts were very large, and also represented a significant increase on those incurred in the previous year. It looked as if £27.8 million of start-up costs on new contracts had completely missed the income statement.

In **Note 11 – Intangible assets** (see opposite), there was £15.5 million of computer software costs, most of which were internally

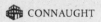 CONNAUGHT

Note 11: Intangible assets, an extract, £m

	Computer software	Research & development expenditure	Acquisition customer relationships	Acquisition computer software	Total
Cost					
At 1 September 2008	8.2	4.5	30.4	5.8	48.9
Additions	9.4	1.9	–	–	11.3
Acquired	–	–	6.3	–	6.3
Disposals	–	(6.4)	–	–	(6.4)
At 31 August 2009	17.6	–	36.7	5.8	60.1
Amortisation					
At 1 September 2008	1.5	1.3	7.9	1.0	11.7
Charged for year	0.6	0.9	7.8	1.2	10.5
Disposals	–	(2.2)	–	–	(2.2)
At 31 August 2009	2.1	–	15.7	2.2	20.0
Net book value					
At 31 August 2009	15.5	–	21.0	3.6	40.1
At 31 August 2008	6.7	3.2	22.5	4.8	37.2

Included within software is internally generated software. All amortisation has been charged to the income statement through administrative expenses. The directors believe the useful life of the development asset to be five years. Other software purchased is amortised over its useful life or four years, whichever is the shorter. Customer relationships represent the value of contracts acquired on the acquisition of subsidiaries and are amortised over the average length of the contracts which is currently 3.25 years.

Included within computer software are **assets under construction of £10.8m** *(2008 £6.9m)*, which have not been amortised as at 31 August 2009 as they have not been brought into use.

Source: 2009 Connaught Annual Report

Employee costs capitalised

Computer system not working

generated, i.e. the company had capitalised the wages and salaries of its own workforce. It looked as if most of this expenditure had been incurred by Connaught over two years. If one assumes that a typical IT employee was being paid £40,000 per annum, that would mean that Connaught had over 190 of its own employees working on an IT project. That is hard to believe, given that this was a social housing contractor, not an IT company. And because the IT systems were apparently not working yet, they were not even being amortised and therefore not being charged as a cost against reported profits.

So one could say that £43.3 million of costs (£15.5 million of employee costs for people who were supposedly working on a new IT system and £27.8 million of supposed start-up costs on new contracts) had bypassed the income statement. In the context of a reported profit of £26.7 million, that is really significant. And that's what one could have seen by taking a cursory look at the company's annual report. There were a great many costs one could not have identified in the annual report, though – like the 50,000 unpaid invoices found in boxes at Connaught's offices in Leeds by the KPMG administrator.

To anyone who had been paying serious attention to the company's accounts, however, it should not have come as a surprise that Connaught went bust in 2010 owing as much as £220 million to lenders and £40 million to unsecured creditors – mostly privately owned small subcontracting businesses who could ill afford not to be paid. Perhaps there had been too many distractions for management: not only was Connaught a sponsor of the National Hunt Cheltenham Festival, it was also sponsoring the chairman's talented son Harry in his efforts to become a racing driver.

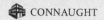

In 2016, some six years after Connaught went bust, the FRC found that allegations of misconduct against the company's auditors, PwC, were justified. These related to, among other things, the work carried out by PwC on mobilisation costs and intangibles at Connaught – which fell significantly short of the standards reasonably expected of an auditor. The finance director of Connaught also admitted that his conduct was sufficiently reckless to amount to acting with a lack of integrity and he was fined and banned from being a chartered accountant for five years.

Lesson

The 2009 Connaught Annual Report was a masterpiece of shop window-dressing. The shop window in 2009 was the income statement in which, written in bright lights, was the rise in operating profits (before goodwill and exceptional items) of 35% to £48.4 million. But the shop window display of increasing profits disguised the fact that many costs were bypassing the income statement and were being recorded out of sight in the store room at the back of the shop – the balance sheet. Big increases in capitalised costs, especially internally generated ones, and long-term receivables are often warning signs that earnings are being overstated.

NCC Group

HUGELY INTANGIBLE

NCC Group, which provides software escrow and verification, and cyber security and managed services, should have been doing so well, what with all the hacking, backdooring, worms, eavesdropping, spoofing, tampering, phishing and goodness knows what else the pesky Ruskies and others get up to. But it was not doing so well back in 2016, which led to subsequent warnings that profits would be below expectations.

The group's first and most precipitous share price dive came that year, when NCC warned that profits would undershoot market forecasts – not so good for a company that only a year earlier in 2015 had raised £126 million at a price of 275p, when trading had apparently been in line with market expectations. There was another profit warning early in 2017 and an admission that the important Assurance Division, which was engaged in the provision of cyber security consulting and professional services, was to be the subject of a strategic review.

NCC continually capitalised costs, including substantial amounts for internally generated software and other development products. All OK as far as accounting standards are concerned, but these were large amounts of costs in the context of expected profits and this accounting treatment kept the expenditure away from the income statement – until one of the company's periodic reassessments of their recoverability, when it was decided that much of what had been previously capitalised was not recoverable at all. Given that their estimates of the recoverability of internally generated software and other development products had been wrong, the periodic profit warnings that followed should not have come as a surprise, since forecasted profits also relied on estimates made by management.

NCC should have been doing so well

NCC describes itself as a ' Global Expert in Cyber Security & Risk Mitigation' and, as its important 2017 Annual Report says, 'In today's threat landscape, understanding the risks your organisation and customers are exposed to is more important than ever.'

Fair enough, but some would also say that understanding the risks to one's investment in NCC shares also needed some consideration. NCC was operating in a hot and topical market – cyber security – but it kept failing to meet expectations. Profit warnings were accompanied by changes in top management. The chairman and chief executive both went. The shares looked as if they had fallen off a cliff – twice. Could we have spotted that there was trouble ahead by scrutinising the 2016 NCC Annual Report? Would there have been enough in it to warn us to steer clear? The simple answer to both questions is 'Yes', and the clues were in **Note 11 – Intangible assets** (see page 29). This note contains the biggest number (£297 million) in the 2016 NCC Annual Report so why wouldn't you want to understand it?

Two profit warnings and two share price dives

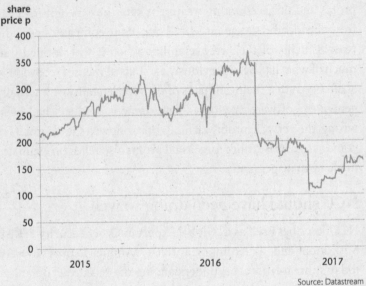

Source: Datastream

Raising money, rising debt

In 2015 there were signs that NCC was not as cash generative as some had thought. Cash was being consumed due to the hefty costs being incurred on developing the company's own software and other development products. In late 2015, NCC raised £126 million by issuing shares at 275p. The company proposed spending £74 million on the initial consideration for the leading Dutch cyber company Fox-IT. There was a further £10.5 million to be paid on each of the first and second anniversaries of the deal. Clearly, NCC was raising much more – £52 million more – than it needed for the initial consideration required for the acquisition of Fox-IT

– and £31 million more than it needed to cover all three payments. This would seem to indicate that cash was being consumed in the business and that the board needed to raise more than just that required to buy Fox-IT, so it wrapped it all up in the financing for the acquisition. Some investors were surprised at the large amount raised, but clearly there were two motives for placing new shares: the acquisition of Fox-IT; and to pay down the £65 million of debt reported in November 2015, which was only getting bigger. Incidentally, NCC paid near enough 55 times after-tax profits and over 5 times sales for Fox-IT – much of which came from a contract with the Dutch government. So Fox-IT was reassuringly expensive and NCC was hoping it was going to be worth it.

An intangibly big number

Intangibles is where NCC recorded nearly £300 million of so-called 'assets' in its 2016 Annual Report. But the trouble was that, every now and then – and rather unexpectedly for investors – NCC had to write them down.

Intangibles included: software that NCC created itself; development costs incurred by, you guessed it, NCC itself; amounts for customer contracts and relationships; and goodwill with values attributed to it that were largely also justified by NCC. There is, of course, nothing wrong with accounting for certain costs in this way, but it does allow such costs to be kept out of the income statement, and therefore the earnings per share figure – which is often all the unsophisticated investor tends to look at.

Take a look at **Note 11 – Intangible assets** (see next page) in the 2016 NCC Annual Report. We know that this is an area of sensitivity that any diligent investor would wish to examine carefully,

Note 11: Intangible assets, an extract, £'000

	Software	Development costs	Customer contracts and relationships	Goodwill	Total
Cost:					
At 1 June 2014	12,943	4,974	23,018	91,651	132,586
Acquisitions through business combinations	340	–	24,581	62,680	87,601
Additions – internally developed	5,075	3,100	–	–	8,175
Effects of movements in exchange rates	–	667	257	1,189	2,113
At 31 May 2015	18,358	8,741	47,856	155,520	230,475
Acquisitions through business combinations	1,706	–	25,393	72,915	100,014
Additions – internally developed	6,944	1,919	–	–	8,863
Costs write down	–	(6,858)	–	–	(6,858)
Effects of movements in exchange rates	(18)	390	2,958	7,705	11,035
At 31 May 2016	26,990	4,192	76,207	236,140	343,529

Development costs finally written down

Large internal development and software costs capitalised

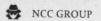

Note 11: Intangible assets, an extract, £'000, continued

	Software	Development costs	Customer contracts and relationships	Goodwill	Total
Accumulated amortisation and impairment losses:					
At 1 June 2014	7,156	–	15,366	–	22,522
Charge for year	**516**	–	2,207	–	2,723
Effects of movement in exchange rates	–	–	294	–	294
At 31 May 2015	**7,672**	–	17,867	–	25,539
Charge for year	1,576	–	6,833	–	8,409
Impairment charge	–	–	–	11,877	11,877
Effects of movements in exchange rates	–	–	427	–	427
At 31 May 2016	**9,248**	–	25,127	11,877	46,252
Net book value:					
At 31 May 2016	**17,742**	**4,192**	**51,080**	**224,263**	**297,277**
At 31 May 2015	**10,686**	**8,741**	**29,989**	**155,520**	**204,936**

Source: 2016 NCC Annual Report

Management have used business forecasts in determining the recoverability of the asset value of software and development costs relating to the creation of new products and services. The remaining useful economic life of customer contracts and relationships is between **2 and 10 years**.

Considerably shorter life than software and development costs	*Very low software amortisation charge*	*Development costs not amortised*

because not only does it contain the largest number in the annual report but also the fastest growing one. The un-amortised intangibles balance grew to £344 million at a compound rate of 35% per annum from 2012 to 2016. Sales may have been growing at a heady 24% per annum, but the growth over the same period in software and development costs that had been capitalised was a much more heady 42% per annum. Alarm bells should already have been ringing and it's here that we need to take a further look.

Note 11 is significant for a number of reasons:

- Development costs never seem to be amortised, so they avoid the income statement altogether.

- In 2016, £6.8 million of development costs were written down following a strategic review through the use of an 'exceptional item'. Always be wary of these, especially if they keep reoccurring, as that would indicate that they may not be exceptional at all. If the development costs had been amortised, this would have been a charge to profits from 2012 to 2016.

- Back in 2012, £6.1 million of software costs were also written off following a decision not to proceed with implementing a new IT system but rather to stick with the company's current IT system. It is a poor indictment indeed when an IT company fails to develop a new IT system for itself that it is supposed to have confidence in.

- An analysis of the historic intangible assets of NCC for the four years up to 2016 show that the capitalised software costs were being amortised over anything from eighteen to forty-five years. Is it credible that capitalised software costs have a useful economic life that long?

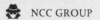

■ In contrast, NCC stated that amounts capitalised in respect of customer contracts and relationships had a useful economic life of between two and ten years. On the basis that software and development costs were incurred for customers where contracts and relationships already existed, surely a more prudent approach would have been to amortise them over the same but shorter period of between two and ten years? There is at least some consistency here.

Lesson

It is always a good idea to understand the biggest number in the accounts – in NCC's case, the intangible assets – and the subjective methods employed in its calculation. The *Pocket Oxford Dictionary* describes an intangible as something 'that is unable to be grasped mentally' or a 'thing that cannot be precisely assessed or defined'. In NCC's case this is entirely relevant, as the company had continually adjusted its value in the past, indicating that earlier estimates were wrong, with the effect that historic profits were overstated. The adjustment to capitalised development costs is quite clear in the NCC 2016 Annual Report published in the middle of that year, so with hindsight no one should have been surprised at the profit warning that came in late 2016 as a result of three large contracts being cancelled, together with a project deferral and problems with a managed service contract. For all of these, estimates were required and NCC already had form for getting its estimates wrong on two previous occasions. However, new management has now been installed and following a strategic review NCC is performing much better.

PART 2

Stock matters

HOW PROFITS CAN BE AFFECTED BY
STOCK VALUE

International Accounting Standard 2 – Inventories (IAS 2), which governs the valuation of inventory, says that it should be valued at the lower of cost and realisable value. If it is not, there can be consequences.

Just ask the investors in Toshiba (see page 234), Royal Doulton, Aero Inventory or Patisserie Holdings (see page 44), the ultimate owner of Patisserie Valerie, if inventory valuations matter. The first three of these companies finally had to confess that their inventory valuations were far too high. The subsequent write-downs caused their share prices to collapse; indeed, the hit to Aero Inventory was so severe that it went bust almost immediately.

Patisserie Holdings had a curiously high valuation for inventories of croissants and black forest gateaux. It was after all a fast food company that had on average over 80 days sales in inventory. The latest count by KPMG, the administrators, indicates a black hole of £96 million. Some of this may have something to do with an overvaluation of inventories. But there will be many other numbers in the accounts that were overstated. It allegedly had shareholders' funds of £99 million so most of this looks to have been wiped out by the fraud.

The Japanese multinational Toshiba had been overstating the value of its inventories of semiconductors and PCs for many years up to 2015 to ensure that the company met expectations. Central management issued so-called 'challenges' to business unit managers specifying the targets they were to meet, often with the threat that certain activities would be closed if they were not. This meant that jobs were on the line and profits were manipulated to meet the challenges. The subsequent adjustment of previous years' profits because of accounting shenanigans caused the share price to fall by 65% in the later part of 2015 and the early part of 2016.

Before it was found out and its share price crashed in 2004, Royal Doulton, the 200-year-old English china manufacturer and figurine maker, had inventory on its balance sheet that was worth eight months of sales. It took new management in the form of the swashbuckling Hamish Grossart to make the necessary accounting adjustments, but frankly anyone who had taken a cursory glance at the company's previous annual reports would have realised that the level of inventory valuation was unsustainable. A write-down and further losses were inevitable. Royal Doulton was taken over by Waterford Wedgwood for a fraction of what it had once been worth in 2004, and then in 2009 Waterford Wedgwood itself went bust. Very few people were buying fine bone china for posh dinner parties, it seems. But couldn't we all have seen that from the huge amounts of inventory on the balance sheets of both these famous names from Britain's great manufacturing past?

How reported profits are affected by inventory valuations, £

Year 1	Closing inventory undervalued		Closing inventory correctly valued		Closing inventory overvalued	
Sales		100		100		100
Opening inventory	20		20		20	
Purchases	60		60		60	
	80		80		80	
Closing inventory	(10)		(20)		(30)	
Cost of goods sold		(70)		(60)		(50)
Gross profit		30		40		50

Year 2	Opening inventory undervalued		Opening inventory correctly valued		Opening inventory overvalued	
Sales		100		100		100
Opening inventory	10		20		30	
Purchases	60		60		60	
	70		80		90	
Closing inventory	(20)		(20)		(20)	
Cost of goods sold		(50)		(60)		(70)
Gross profit		**50**		40		**30**
Total gross profit for years 1 and 2		80		80		80

Undervalued closing inventory in Year 1 means greater profits in Year 2

Overvalued closing inventory in Year 1 means smaller profits in Year 2

It was seemingly flying along so well at Aero Inventory – a supplier of commercial aircraft parts. In 2009, the year that its shares were suspended, the company raised new equity at 250p on the back of a large spare parts order from Air Canada. Aero Inventory even had plans to move from AIM to a full listing on the main market of the London Stock Exchange. But then disaster struck. Due diligence ahead of the listing move revealed a substantial overvaluation of inventory. This was so bad that the bankers withdrew their support. Stock matters, you see.

But stock can be undervalued as well as overvalued. What happens if inventory valuations are too low – in other words, below the cost or net realisable value? The answer is that, in the accounting period that the inventory is written down, a loss will be recorded of the amount of the write-down in the income statement. But in the subsequent accounting period, if the inventory is sold for more than its written-down value, a profit will be recorded.

The relationship between stock value and profits is best illustrated in a table such as the one on the previous page, which shows how profits can be shifted from one period to another by changing the value of closing stock in Year 1 but keeping all other items the same. Remember, one year's closing stock is the next year's opening stock. Undervalued inventory in Year 1 means Year 2 benefits in terms of profits. Overvalued inventory in Year 1 means Year 2 suffers in terms of profits. So again, stock valuations matter. Sports Direct made an out-of-the-ordinary downward adjustment to stock in the year before its Initial Public Offering (IPO) in 2007, which was worthy of investigation at the time.

Sports Direct

TAKING STOCK

Mike Ashley, who was a very useful squash player until he got injured, opened his first sports shop in Maidenhead in 1982. He expanded rapidly but remained a sole trader until he incorporated his business in 1999. Eight years later, in 2007, he raised £929 million when he sold a minority stake in his company, Sports Direct, following its flotation on the London Stock Exchange (LSE) through an IPO. That gave him enough money to spend around £135 million on buying Newcastle United FC, with plenty to spare.

But it was not long before Sports Direct, the owner of brands like Kangol, Dunlop, Karrimor, Donnay and Slazenger, was disappointing investors who had bought shares at the time of the IPO. Little more than six months after its shares were listed on the LSE, the company warned that it was not going to meet the profit expectations that the keen City of London analysts had inked in for the following years. Perhaps they would not have been so bullish if they had analysed the chances of England qualifying for the 2008 UEFA European Championship. Three lions on a white football shirt sell much better when England's finest are playing well and, if England had qualified, shirt sales would have helped Sports Direct get closer to meeting expectations.

But they really also should have spent more time analysing the Sports Direct IPO prospectus, which showed some helpful numbers that could have indicated that future profit forecasts were going to be tough to meet. In the investors' eyes, missing short-term profit expectations so soon after an IPO is unforgivable, and it was not until five years later that the Sports Direct share price finally reached 300p, the price at which Mike Ashley had originally sold shares to new investors at the IPO.

Mike Ashley is a controversial and unconventional figure who has his admirers and, although an investment in Sports Direct may have felt like a ride on a roller coaster, no one can deny that the company has shaken up the UK's retailing industry. The group has purchased troubled retailers such as House of Fraser, Evans Cycles, Game Digital, Jack Wills and Sofa.com. A stake was acquired in Debenhams, which has since gone bust, and stakes in French Connection and Goals Soccer Centres have also not been good investments. Many feel that Sports Direct's acquisition spree on the high street is badly timed as online continues to grow and business rates remain high. It seems Mike Ashley cannot resist a flutter on the high street but the bets are just bigger than those made in London casinos. Meanwhile the company's auditors, Grant Thornton, have resigned following the disclosure of a €674m tax bill from the Belgian authorities. Not surprising then that Sports Direct's share price was below its original IPO price of 300p.

From excitement to disappointment

There's nothing much better than reading an IPO prospectus for getting under the skin of a company. Very rarely will investors be in possession of this level of detail again, so the prospectus should be used to glean as much information as possible before deciding to invest. Of course, the rushed way listings were brought to the market in 2007 (and still are) afforded little time to read a full prospectus before an answer was required from the lead broker in the IPO syndicate as to whether potential investors wanted any shares or not. But there isn't really any excuse if, after the IPO, the share price disappoints based perhaps on information that was in the prospectus all along.

The year of its flotation was a bumper year for Sports Direct, but it wasn't long before management were dampening down analysts' enthusiasm and forecasts for future periods. The AGM Statement in September 2007, only some six months after the IPO, said that '2008 should show limited growth'. The Trading Statement in November 2007 said that 'EBITDA [Earnings before Interest, Taxes, Depreciation and Amortisation] for the current financial year was likely to be below that achieved in the last year'. Those who had invested at the IPO were not amused when Sports Direct reported underlying profits of £85 million in 2008, a fall of 51% from those reported just after the flotation. In 2007 the company reported underlying profits of £174 million.

Sports Direct's share price continued its dive following these disappointing announcements, losing nearly 90% of its value in spite of the fact that the company kept buying back its own shares in the market in a vain attempt to halt the slide. The shares plunged, perhaps not as dramatically as a high cliff diver of Acapulco over

Share price swallow dives after flotation

share price p

Source: Datastream

that period, more like a swallow diver. At its nadir the share price reached 32p. Since then Sports Direct has been a bumpy ride for shareholders as the market has reacted to its fortunes and strategic shifts and some unprofitable investments under Mike Ashley's firm but unpredictable control. That said, Sports Direct has become a category killer in its space, which big brands like Nike and adidas cannot afford to ignore.

Taking stock

As any fresh-faced newly qualified accountant will tell you, stock valuations at the end and at the beginning of accounting periods matter hugely, especially for retailers. This is because if you want

Note 17: Inventories, £'000

	52 weeks ended 25 April 2004	52 weeks ended 24 April 2005	53 weeks ended 30 April 2006	26 weeks ended 29 October 2006
Raw materials	8,871	3,821	2,024	3,399
Work in progress	4,624	3,544	794	1,252
Goods for resale	113,279	152,651	215,990	205,318
	126,774	160,016	218,808	209,969

The following inventory write-downs have been recognised in cost of sales:

	52 weeks ended 25 April 2004	52 weeks ended 24 April 2005	53 weeks ended 30 April 2006	26 weeks ended 29 October 2006
Inventory write-down charge	2,101	5,904	20,225	5,340

Source: 2007 Sports Direct Prospectus

Unusually large inventory write-down in year before IPO

to maximise profits in an accounting period it is best to have a high valuation for stock at the end of the period, or conversely a low valuation of stock at the beginning. As one year's closing stock is the next year's opening stock, you can't have your cake and eat it – but what is beyond doubt is that stock valuations can be helpful in determining profits and in which period they are reported. Take a look at **Note 17 – Inventories** (above) extracted from the 2007 Sports Direct Prospectus, made widely available to all potential investors, if only for a limited period.

Perhaps some articulated lorries stuffed with sports goods went missing, or maybe it was all that 'shrinkage' caused by the workers in the Sports Direct warehouse in Shirebrook, Derbyshire that required the £20 million inventory write-down charge, but the unusualness of the size of the write-down stands out when compared with the much smaller adjustments made in previous years. So why was there such a large downward revision in the valuation of Nike and adidas trainers and other sports goods just ahead of the flotation of Sports Direct?

There may have been a completely legitimate explanation for the revision but it is not given in the prospectus and, because of this adjustment, it could be said that Sports Direct entered the year of the flotation – for the year ending April 2007 – with £20 million of stock valued at zero. A cursory look at the company's income statement at that time reveals that the mark-up on sports items such as trainers and football shirts at Sports Direct was 70%. Marking up £20 million of stock by 70% gives £34 million of sales that potentially have no direct cost attached. There was, then, potentially £34 million of extra profit that might not have been reported in the year of flotation without this write-down on inventory in the previous year. Of course, this does not explain all of the difference between the £174 million underlying profits reported in 2007 and the disappointing profits of £85 million reported in 2008. However, for anyone who noticed the unusually large stock write-down, this alone should have dampened their enthusiasm for Sports Direct's shares at its IPO and caused them to investigate the reason for it.

Lesson

The balance sheet is always worth inspecting ahead of an IPO. Remember, it is very often in the bankers' and advisers' interests

to maximise the valuation of the company, as their fees may depend on it – and that often means maximising near-term profits, perhaps at the expense of profits further out. Any unusual reduction in asset valuations for items such as inventory, receivables and fixed assets ahead of a flotation may help boost the next set of profits but it may well also make it difficult to achieve the targets inked in for future periods.

Patisserie Holdings

NOT EVERYONE LIKES CAKES

'Everyone likes cakes!' That was what a senior director of RHM, the owner of Mr Kipling and every granny's favourite cake company – since purchased by Premier Foods – once said during the flotation of his company on the London Stock Exchange. A quick look at how the shares of both Patisserie Holdings (the owner of Patisserie Valerie) and Premier Foods have done since then would indicate that actually not everyone likes cakes at all. Patisserie Holdings has gone bust because of a fraud and Premier Foods limps on as a public company saddled with debt taken on as a result of its ill-planned acquisition spree, including the purchase of Mr Kipling itself.

But Patisserie Valerie, established in Soho in 1926 by a Belgian couple called Esther van Gyseghem and Theo Vermeirsch, was doing so well following its purchase by Luke Johnson's Risk Capital Partners in 2006. Well, that's what the annual reports of Patisserie Holdings told us. It was apparently successfully rolling out the 'much-loved institution' that is Patisserie Valerie across the nation, taking delightfully named cakes including Angelica

Gateaux, Obsession Gateaux, Black Forest Gateaux and Demi Mousses to the older generations living in well-to-do areas up and down the country. Apparently, everyone was indulging in freshly baked premium cakes and patisseries and enjoying quality teas and coffees served from over 150 cafés. Patisserie Holdings also owned other nascent brands, some of which some said had the potential to be as successful as Patisserie Valerie itself, including Druckers, a Viennese cake shop, Philpotts, an upmarket gourmet sandwich shop, Baker & Spice, a high-end deli and Flour Power City, an artisan bakery based in Lewisham. Patisserie Holdings it seemed had every intention of wanting to dominate the high-end cake and artisan bread markets just as Greggs dominated the other end. But these two companies could not have been more different.

The 2017 Patisserie Holdings Annual Report highlighted how well trading was going – unbelievably well apparently. On the basis that pictures speak louder than words, graphs or histograms showing key performance indicators (KPIs) are commonly used by company directors to demonstrate how well trading has gone in any given period, and Luke Johnson and his fellow directors at Patisserie Valerie were no exception. The highlights page in the 2017 Patisserie Holdings Annual Report pictured revenues, gross profit, net profit and EBITDA advancing steadily in graph form, from bottom left to top right at an angle of about 30 degrees and because the 'y' axis was squashed, in order to fit these vital messages on one page, these important KPI progressions looked consistent year after year – see **Highlights** (next page). There were no wobbles in the Patisserie Valerie track record, confirming, or so it seemed, that the Patisserie Valerie concept was a successful roll-out that could just keep growing consistently into new areas in the UK and perhaps even overseas. New Patisserie Valerie cafés

Highlights – an extract, £m

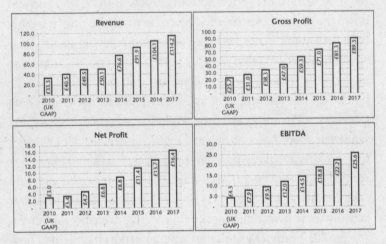

Source: 2017 Patisserie Holdings Annual Report

were apparently profitable from their very first week of trading, which made it look as if the company was able to finance its own growth without recourse to shareholders for more money. Patisserie Valerie was apparently selling hot cakes. But wasn't it too good to be true? We now know that it was all lies.

Schadenfreude

One of the last bits of good news from the company came in May 2018, when its executive chairman, Luke Johnson, proudly announced a record set of interim results and highlighted that there was £29 million of cash on the balance sheet.

Five months later the shares were suspended. There was actually no cash on the balance sheet, only debt. There were potentially fraudulent accounting irregularities and, perhaps not surprisingly, the finance director was arrested. There were also stories of bouncing cheques, forged signatures and fictitious invoices. Oh, and the FRC, the accountants' regulator, and the SFO were to investigate the company. Quite a fall from grace for Patisserie Valerie and the high-profile chairman of its holding company Patisserie Holdings, who was never shy of telling anyone who wanted to listen that his way of running businesses was the best. He loved sounding off in his *Sunday Times* column about how many of us were financially illiterate and about tried and tested swindles. There was, not surprisingly, considerable schadenfreude when the company in which he had a large stake, and of which he was executive chairman, went bust. Running a business is not quite the cakewalk Luke Johnson said it was. The Patisserie Valerie chain has since been purchased by a private equity firm called Causeway for a mere £13 million. A far cry indeed from the value given to its holding company, Patisserie Holdings, by investors of nearly £500 million in 2018.

Very stale cakes and croissants

As with many company disasters, the signs were there in the accounts of Patisserie Holdings that things were not quite as good as depicted. There were certainly some odd financial metrics that stood out like cherries on the top of a Schwarzwaelder Kirsch Torte.

- Firstly, whilst apparently there was plenty of cash (nearly £29 million) on the balance sheet, there was no interest income from it. Usually companies place excess cash on deposit and earn interest on it, but there was none at Patisserie Holdings.
- Margins were very high. In the last set of results that the company reported, operating margins were over 18%. To put

Shares suspended at nearly their peak

Source: Datastream

this into context, similar companies like Restaurant Group report operating margins of 8% and Costa Coffee report operating margins of 12%. There will of course be plenty of reasons for the differences between these companies but Patisserie Valerie's margins were so high compared with other restaurant chains that some explanation should have been given by the company – or requested by investors. But there was another number that said that you cannot have your cake and eat it.

Keen number crunchers know that the closing stock or inventory valuation number is key in determining the profits of a company. The higher the closing inventory valuation, the more profits a company reports as this is a deduction from costs. This is why auditors should spend time checking the valuation and why they should attend stock checks at a company's year end to ensure it is correct.

Half-year to 31 March, an extract, £'000

	2018	2017	Year to 30 Sep 2017
Inventories	5,990	4,901	5,980
Cost of sales	13,465	12,188	24,931
Average age of inventory	**81 days**	**73 days**	**87 days**

Very old croissants!

Source: 2018 Patisserie Holdings half-year report

That inventory valuations were very high at Patisserie Holdings was an obvious warning sign to be cautious about the shares. Its main subsidiary was Patisserie Valerie – it would not have liked this downmarket description but it is a fast food retailer. We can expect that coffee was freshly ground and cakes and pastries were freshly prepared and baked at Patisserie Valerie, surely? Not so, according to a string of results released prior to the company going bust, that reported large amounts of inventory. In the last set of results, for instance, before the company went bust, there was £6 million of inventory – see **Half-year to 31 March** (above) from the 2018 Patisserie Valerie half-year report above. Why on earth, you might have asked, has the company got so much inventory, which will include cakes, on its balance sheet? To put this in context, the cost of sales of coffees, croissants and cakes at Patisserie Holdings was £13.5 million for the six months before it went bust. This means that the average age of inventory then was some 81 days, which must have meant that the company had a huge number of very stale cakes and mouldy croissants in its stores. In fact, some of the cakes may have been rock hard as they were possibly over 160 days old! In contrast, Costa Coffee has inventories of cakes and croissants that are 28 days old – still quite old but probably explained by some being frozen.

Lesson

Frauds are very difficult to spot just by looking at an annual report. They are particularly hard to spot if there has been collusion amongst others. In addition to the finance director, Chris Marsh, who was arrested but released on bail, five others at Patisserie Holdings were arrested in a joint operation involving the SFO and the police. Those who understand the dynamics of fast food retailing should know that inventory generally is fresh and therefore having some stock that is largely perishable but possibly as old as 160 days stretches credibility. In view of the importance of the value of stock in determining profits, investors need to determine how many days of sales are in stock. Too many days often means there is an obsolescence issue at best and perhaps worse as was the case at Patisserie Holdings. In addition to the fact that no interest was being earned on the reported large cash balances and that margins were way ahead of its comparator companies, this was a clear sign that something was not quite right.

PART 3

Promises and estimates

THE DIFFICULTIES WITH ACCRUALS

A telltale sign that a company may be due for a devastatingly big fall in its share price is the inclusion of large amounts of accrued income (estimated expected revenue) in its balance sheet. Simple analysis often also reveals that the companies that accrue large amounts of income wait a long time for their money, meaning that their cash flow can be poor – a prime reason companies go bust. Just ask investors in Australian law firm Slater and Gordon, Hewlett-Packard (HP) and two UK software companies, iSoft and Cedar Group, who took a hammering when their share prices dived. There are others, many of which were in the IT sector, where in the past UK accounting regulations allowed revenue to be recognised once software has been delivered to the client. US Generally Accepted Accounting Principles (US GAAP) also allowed this at one time. Clearly in some cases the delivery of a software product indicates when the relationship with the client commences, but often there is still much to do, as the software needs to be both implemented and tested, and this process can sometimes take years. Surely, therefore, some argued, the software sale should be recognised as taking place over the period of the implementation – and in general terms this is what International Financial Reporting Standards (IFRS) have directed. When this revenue recognition change came, it devastated the profits of some companies and put them at risk of breaching their banking covenants.

International Accounting Standard 1 (IAS 1) sets out how financial reporting statements should be prepared. One of the key accounting concepts included in IAS 1 is that a company should prepare its financial statements using the accruals method of accounting. This means that financial statements are prepared on the basis that transactions are recorded not as cash is received or paid but as the income is earned or as the expense is incurred in the period to which it relates. Also, when calculating profits, the income earned must be matched with the expenses incurred in generating them. The application of the accruals concept should result in the accurate reporting of income and expenses, assets and liabilities, and therefore of profits, which enables the user of financial statements to analyse the performance and financial position of a company.

The trouble with the accruals basis of accounting, however, is that a great deal of judgement is required on the part of management to implement it and this can make the auditor's job difficult in deciding whether that judgement is justifiable. Whereas cash accounting – that is, accounting for transactions when cash is received or paid – is relatively simple, accruals accounting is more complicated and more open to abuse. It can allow sales and revenues to be overstated and costs understated, and provides an easy way for profits to be massaged up or down. Remember that accrued income in a company's balance sheet is un-invoiced income and is therefore only an estimate of what the company thinks it is owed.

In 2015, the Australian law firm Slater and Gordon was presumably happy with its acquisition when it purchased a personal injury business from the UK company Quindell, despite the inclusion in the 2013 Quindell Annual Report of a massive accrued income balance of £152 million (much of it relating to the personal injury business Slater and Gordon had acquired). The amount was equal to 40% of that year's sales for Quindell.

In 2000, the underwriters of business software company Cedar Group's failed rights issue seemingly were happy that much of its software sales for the year were accounted for as a massive accrual of income.

In 2004, iSoft investors were presumably happy that a third of sales were not invoiced but accrued for. Remember that software sales have very little cost of sale, so the vast majority of this accrual would have been recorded as pure profit. In the context of a profit before tax of £17 million reported by iSoft that year, a revenue accrual of £50 million is a massive one, without which losses would have been reported.

Some shareholders in the multinational tech company HP were never happy that it bought the Cambridge-based software company Autonomy, but the deal went ahead anyway – Autonomy was one of many very poor acquisitions that the company made. There were red flags in the 2010 Autonomy Annual Report that should have warned HP to do thorough due diligence, though curiously we cannot say that this included the extent of accrued income – Autonomy stopped disclosing an accrued income balance back in 2004. But at this time many software companies accrued income on sales and we can only assume it was tucked away in 'Trade or other receivables'. Anyway, Autonomy was waiting on average three months for its money – sufficient reason alone to raise questions about revenue recognition, especially as accrued income was not disclosed.

A more recent IT company disaster was Redcentric which collapsed in 2016. The 2016 Redcentric Annual Report was a masterpiece of window dressing. The window dressing included big increases in prepayments, trade receivables and of course accrued income. Trade payables rose too and cash had been over-stated. But it should have been clear to those who bothered to look at the 2016 Redcentric Annual Report that these large increases did not sit easily alongside the much more modest rise in sales.

There were shocks from Utilitywise, an energy broker that made some very optimistic assumptions about the commissions it expected to receive from its suppliers for lining up contracts for them. But the signs were there that the light would go out on the share price when in 2015 the discount rate employed to calculate the present value of expected commissions was suddenly reduced from 9% to 3%, a level that was not justified – and it was not long before Utilitywise was backtracking on its forecasts.

Investors should have heeded the observation made by Benjamin Franklin in 1839 that the 'great part of the miseries of mankind were brought upon them by the false estimates they had made of the value of things'.

Hewlett-Packard and Autonomy

BUYER BE WARY

A staggering $25 billion! This was the loss that accrued to shareholders in Hewlett-Packard (HP) between the appointment of Léo Apotheker as CEO in 2010 and the admission by his successor, Meg Whitman, a year later that they had paid $8.8 billion too much for the UK's largest software company at the time, Autonomy. But for many it was not a matter of if HP would ever confess to the blunder, but when. HP was well practised at making value-destroying acquisitions, but it was surprising that it got Autonomy so wrong so quickly. Mind you, its 2002 purchase of hardware producer Compaq was not a bed of roses either, and neither was Electronic Data Systems (EDS), which it acquired in 2008. Odd, really, as one would have thought that these companies had been acquired only following appropriate and extensive due diligence – especially by a company whose board at the time was stuffed full of the great and the good of corporate America. Only later was the world to find out that the HP board was riven by rivalries, bickering and leaks to the press – hardly a contented board that was able to formulate the right strategy and make acquisition decisions for the company.

New management and Autonomy hit HP share price

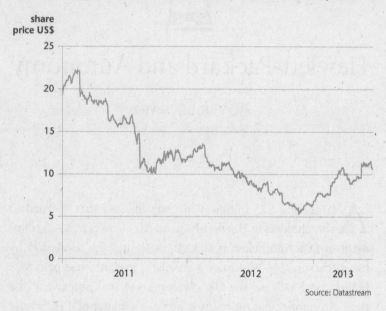

share
price US$

Source: Datastream

Whilst the acquisitions of Compaq, EDS and indeed Palm were a mixed bunch as far as adding shareholder value was concerned, they did not have the devastating impact of the acquisition of Autonomy, and the arrival of Léo Apotheker as CEO, on the shares of HP. Léo who? Many people had never heard of Léo Apotheker when he was appointed to lead HP, and some certainly struggled to pronounce his name – LAY-o AH-pothecker. The new CEO of HP was a German businessman who was fluent in five languages, but he had no experience of the company's main line of business – computer hardware and printers.

HP was floundering. From its beginnings in a tiny garage in Palo Alto, California, in 1938, HP had grown to become the world's largest PC maker. But HP did not have enough geeks working for it. Under Lew Platt it had missed the internet opportunity, and under Carly Fiorina it had made too many uninspiring acquisitions. Mark Hurd, her successor, was credited with some recovery by slashing costs, but had to make a hasty exit in 2010 after an expenses investigation. Following on from him, Léo Apotheker's remit was to improve the performance of HP by focusing more on growing new markets such as software, the cloud and mobile. Past acquisitions and its strategy had failed to reposition the company sufficiently to improve the performance of its shares. Apotheker, who had previously been running a German software firm called SAP, was the leader chosen to transform the fortunes of HP. He certainly did that! But he did not last one year at the helm of HP, leaving involuntarily even before his brainchild deal with Autonomy was completed. He had lost the confidence of the board and other key HP executives, and during his very short tenure the share price had halved. But his legacy continued well after he left, as the shareholder value destruction continued from the decision to buy Autonomy that was made on his watch.

Autonomy – another value-destroying acquisition

In August 2011, HP announced that it was in discussions to buy Autonomy – a controversial decision in the eyes of many of its followers. It ultimately paid cash of £25.50 per share, a massive 70% premium to the share price ahead of the bid, or $11 billion in total, which was 50 times historic earnings or nearly 13 times historic sales – in other words, Autonomy was a very expensive acquisition. Even though HP's CFO Cathy Lesjak was against the acquisition of Autonomy, it went ahead. At the same time

HP announced that it was lowering its earnings forecast for that year, pulling out of tablets and mobile phones, and it was going to demerge its large PC business. There was a lot going on at HP, it seemed. The shares tanked 10% on the day of these announcements. A month later, in September 2011, Léo Apotheker was fired, leaving his replacement, Meg Whitman, to pick up the many pieces of a failed acquisition strategy going back years. She had a record of slashing valuations and she was quick to evaluate the legacy of previous acquisitions. Within a year of her arrival at HP, she had taken a knife to their balance sheet valuations. She made the deepest cut to Autonomy's valuation, but she had sharpened her knife on the EDS and Compaq acquisitions made in previous periods. HP had paid a top price of $11.0 billion for Autonomy but was now saying that it was worth only $2.2 billion – $8.8 billion less than the acquisition price. Some $5.7 billion of the reduction related to alleged accounting irregularities that had been uncovered, which meant that revenues in the future would grow at a much slower rate than had been originally expected. The other $3.1 billion of the reduction in value was the result of a newly reduced estimate of the value of intangibles in Autonomy's own balance sheet.

What many in the market had always expected was coming to pass. Having had Autonomy in the group for just over a year, HP now had to confess that it had paid far too much for it. But HP should have known all about Autonomy before buying it. Few UK investors would go anywhere near the company and its accounts looked odd – well, a bit like Cedar Group's and iSoft's (see pages 63 and 69), to be precise – both of which had seen their share prices collapse because of accounting irregularities. What was the extent of due diligence at HP? Superficial is probably the right answer.

HP's major acquisitions and impairments –
2002 to 2012, $ billion

Target	Cost	Impairment
Autonomy	11.0	8.8
EDS	14.0	8.0
Compaq	24.0	1.2
Palm	1.2	0.9

Source: FT research, HP

The regulators both in the UK and the US have been busy. In 2013 the Financial Reporting Council (FRC) announced an investigation into the accounts of Autonomy and the audit work carried out by its auditors, Deloitte. After five years, the FRC has concluded that it believes there are formal complaints in connection with the conduct of Deloitte, the two partners that conducted the audit of the company and two finance personnel at Autonomy. The formal complaints levelled by the FRC revolve around the financial reporting of Autonomy between 1st January 2009 and 30th June 2011, and allege that the conduct of the parties fell significantly short of the standards reasonably expected. The FRC move follows legal proceedings in the US that resulted in the conviction for fraud and five-year prison sentence for Autonomy's finance director. The finance director was also sentenced to an additional three years of supervised release and ordered to pay a $4 million fine and a forfeiture payment of $6.1 million. He is appealing the conviction. Meanwhile, in 2019 former Autonomy chief executive Mike Lynch found himself in the High Court in London in a £5bn civil lawsuit following criminal charges for conspiracy and fraud levelled by the US Department of Justice relating to the purchase of his company by HP. It seems that the investigative wheels of the US Securities and Exchange Commission (SEC) and the black suits of the Federal Bureau of Investigation (FBI) turn considerably faster than those of the FRC in the UK and certainly hit harder. The FRC has yet to opine!

Small red flags

It is difficult to pinpoint one large red flag in the 2010 Autonomy Annual Report that should have deterred HP from acquiring the company, or at least encouraged it to undertake a thorough due diligence exercise. There was, however, a semaphore of small red flags that together spelt out danger. For instance:

- There was the $1.4 billion of goodwill on the balance sheet that was difficult to justify, as there was only one cash-generating unit (CGU) – Autonomy itself. All acquisitions were rapidly integrated into the group and therefore the CGUs derived from the acquisitions apparently were not identifiable.

- In the two years ending 2010 there was $63 million of internal costs that were capitalised as internally generated assets, in other words capitalised research and development (R&D) – nothing wrong with this, but worthy of investigation given the amount.

- Patents, licences and trademarks, R&D, purchased technology, customer relationships and brand names with a value of $400 million were all held as assets on the balance sheet at the end of 2010 and were depreciated from between one and ten years – ten years is a long time in the world of IT.

- A large provision of $11.4 million was made on the acquisition of another software company, Interwoven, in 2009. Provisions can be helpful to defray normal running costs away from the income statement – and so this, too, should have been worthy of investigation.

- Autonomy was taking three to four months to collect its cash from clients in 2010. This may of course have been due to slow payers – often governments or public bodies – but that is a long time and raises questions about revenue recognition. This is always something worth checking with software companies and from the evidence submitted in the courts in the UK and the US, this is an area that interested prosecutors in particular.

- Depreciation, a cost to the income statement, on tangible fixed assets fell between 2009 and 2010, although fixed asset costs actually rose in the period. This is odd, as one usually sees depreciation rise roughly in line with fixed asset costs.

- Deferred revenue is a store of future revenue. In general, it should rise in line with sales over time. However, in Autonomy's case in 2010 it was pretty much flat, although sales rose by 18% in that year – worthy of some explanation.

- In 2010, Autonomy purchased a leading reseller of its products, MicroLink LLC, which targeted US state and federal government accounts. Autonomy paid $76 million for this company together with Computer Associates Inc's information governance business. These businesses had no net assets and neither were they materially profitable. When a company buys a distributor of its own products it is always worthy of further investigation.

Lesson

There was plenty of stuff to get one's forensic teeth into in the 2010 Autonomy Annual Report. Individually, each issue would have been worthy of enquiry and probably dismissal as an odd quirk of the business itself following discussion with the management of the company. But, rather like a jigsaw puzzle, where it is difficult to discern the picture from one piece, it is only when the pieces are carefully put together that the image reveals itself. There were many pieces to the accounting jigsaw that, when pieced together, showed the full picture at Autonomy ... a big red flag.

Cedar Group

TIMBER!

In 2002 Cedar reported losses of £181 million on sales of just £86 million. That takes some doing. But prior to this, just for a very short time, Cedar was everyone's favourite software company – well, certainly in the Surrey town of Cobham, home of Chelsea football players, stockbrokers and Cedar itself.

If the residents of Cobham had bought some Cedar shares towards the beginning of 1999 and sold them in the early part of 2000, when they were at their peak, they would have made some seventeen times what they had invested. Mind you, anyone who bought shares in any old IT company then, especially ones that sold software, would have made large profits as the tech bubble inflated in 1999 and the early part of 2000. The trouble with many of these companies, though, was that like Cedar they were overstating their profits. Any paper gains on tech stocks over that short period were largely wiped out when the tech bubble burst and some software companies were forced to adopt more conservative accounting policies for revenue recognition.

Cedar sold customer relationship management software systems and services which allowed companies to track the activities of their customers. Cedar was acquisitive and often raised finance through the placing of shares to make purchases of similar software companies both in the UK and North America. Cedar's last financing deal was a rights issue in 2000, which ended in disaster when the new shares were left with the underwriters as investors finally began to fret about the company's accounting. A failed rights issue such as this – which happens when the share price falls below the rights issue price – was almost unheard of in investment circles at that time.

Cedar clearly had its fans for a while and reached the heady heights of 1474p before falling to just 3p, at which point it was taken over by Alchemy, a venture capital firm headed by the highly experienced Jon Moulton.

Timber!

Source: Datastream

Rumbled and tumbled

The aggressive accounting that had allowed revenue to be recognised well ahead of cash being received was rumbled, unhelpfully for Cedar, in the middle of a rights issue to raise money for an acquisition. The shares subsequently tumbled. Cedar employed more aggressive accounting methods than most, but it was not alone in overstating profits – many of the UK's leading software companies were at it, as a result of which there were some spectacular blow-ups: AIT, Anite, Recognition Systems and, eventually, iSoft all fell to earth. At this heady time for tech stocks, many rather hopefully promoted themselves as the UK's answer to Oracle and Microsoft.

Cedar was special in that it went spectacularly wrong very quickly. The rights issue failed because Cedar's management had finally lost the confidence of its investors and, without the capital that bankers and investors had happily hitherto provided, its debts mounted up. A year later, following the combination of the adoption of much more prudent accounting policies and a slowdown in its markets, Cedar reported losses of a massive £181 million for the year ended March 2002, for which analysts had originally forecast profits of £24 million.

The shares that had enjoyed a peak of nearly 1500p in 2000 finally traded at just 5p in early 2002, when Alchemy bought those held by institutional investors. The thousands of small investors who thought the 5p a share being offered by Alchemy was derisory ended up having to accept 3p a share in 2003 – a lesson indeed for minority shareholders, some of them very likely residents of Cobham.

There were a number of telltale signs that all was not well in the 2000 Cedar Group Annual Report. For example, Cedar was very acquisitive (it even bought its own US distributor – possibly to avoid a large bad debt); the company kept raising finance via placings and rights issues; it paid bonuses without accounting for the additional National Insurance Contribution; and Cedar did not generate cash.

Aggressive revenue recognition

But what was most striking about Cedar was its revenue recognition policy and how this manifested itself in **Note 14 – Debtors** (see next page) in its 2000 Annual Report. This tells us that the company may have been booking sales way ahead of delivering and installing its product, and certainly in advance of receiving any cash. It can be clearly seen from this note that Cedar was taking on average 281 days, or over nine months, to collect cash owed to it by its clients in 2000. And if 281 days was the average cash collection period, then there must have been some clients who were taking even longer to pay – a completely unsustainable situation that Cedar's bankers and shareholders were unlikely to support with increased loans and equity finance for ever. Unless you have massive margins and can afford to finance your own growth, there are very few companies that can run a business for any length of time with this long a cash collection period, especially in a fast-growing market. This was enough of a warning sign in itself to scare off investors and one that probably put off many during the doomed rights issue in 2000.

A mad scramble for sales before the year end

It's not unusual for companies to scramble around for sales at the

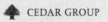

Note 14: Debtors, an extract, £'000

	2000	1999
Amounts falling due within one year:		
Trade debtors	**9,531**	**7,259**
Accrued revenue	**18,505**	**9,177**
Prepayments	1,635	469
Amounts due from subsidiary undertakings	–	–
ACT recoverable	–	252
Other debtors	434	68
Restricted cash	57	2,583
	30,162	19,808
Amounts falling due after one year:		
ACT recoverable	–	67
NIC recoverable from staff	2,642	–
	2,642	67

Source: 2000 Cedar Group Annual Report

	2000	1999
Trade debtors	9,531	7,259
Accrued revenue	18,505	9,177
	28,036	16,436
Annual sales	36,314	23,046
Debtors' turnover period	281 days	260 days

year end. But for software companies such as Cedar there was even more frenetic activity, as management needed to hit market expectations and IT salesmen needed to hit their targets in order for their bonuses to be paid. Remember, software licence sales are almost pure profit as there is virtually no cost of sale, so no wonder there was such pressure for licences to be sold and out of the door by the year end. The analysis below shows that just about all of Cedar's accrued income in 2000 may have related to the sale of software licences, indicating a mad scramble at the year end to get the deals done.

Large amounts of accrued income

	2000	1999
Sales of licences, £m	18.10	9.90
Accrued income, £m	18.51	9.18
Accrued income/sales of licences, %	102	93

Source: 2000 Cedar Group Annual Report

A mad scramble to get sales of software licences done at year end

Lesson

If a company is waiting a long time for its money, that probably means its clients do not think they owe it, or at any rate, not yet. In this scenario there will often be trouble ahead – which was certainly true for Cedar. The 2000 Cedar Group Annual Report was particularly unusual in that it showed accrued income (revenue included in the income statement but not yet invoiced) as being significantly higher than trade receivables (revenue that had been invoiced but was still outstanding at the year end). In fact, accrued income was nearly twice the size of trade receivables. Large amounts of accrued income, especially in software companies, are worth investigating thoroughly.

iSoft

HARD LANDING

It was a mystery to many that the management at iSoft took so long to come clean on their profit numbers. The end of the tech boom in 2000 and 2001 saw a number of companies, such as Cedar Group (see page 63), confess that they had been aggressive in the way they recognised profits from sales of software. But iSoft only came clean in 2006, and when it did, the share price plunged, losing 90% of its value. For many readers of iSoft's accounts back in the day, it seemed that it was only a matter of time before the shares crash landed, but for years the auditors signed off large amounts of accrued income derived from the sale of software, which kept both profits and the share price puffed up.

The big daddy of iSoft was accountant and Barnsley FC owner Patrick Cryne. In 1998 he and three chums – the youthful Tim Whiston, prominent Birmingham businessman Roger Dickens and IT consultant Stephen Graham – teamed up to buy a healthcare software business from KPMG, which they called iSoft. The four had a couple of things in common – they were alumni of KPMG and/or they were accountants. This chummy management team created a leading UK IT software company that was at the centre of the project to upgrade the NHS computer systems alongside giant IT companies like Accenture, Fujitsu and Computer Sciences Corporation (CSC). Following the all share merger with its main competitor Torex in 2004, iSoft felt that it would be more than able to deliver what the NHS wanted for its IT system. The aim of the National Programme for Information Technology (NPfIT) at the NHS – perhaps the largest civil IT project ever – was to computerise all UK patient records and link 30,000 doctors with 300 hospitals in a secure way. The programme has since been abandoned, at a cost of at least £10 billion to the UK taxpayer so far, and probably more to come. iSoft was part of this débâcle.

At its peak in 2005, iSoft was worth over £1 billion. It was a stock market darling that a former Confederation of British Industry (CBI) president, Lord Digby Jones of Birmingham, decided was good enough to lend his name to as a non-executive director. But why also did the experienced Gavin James of Morse Group join as finance director? I remember asking him why he took the job soon after he arrived – when he already had the look of a man who wished he had done more due diligence. A few phone calls to the right people and a glance at the balance sheet would have sufficed. Not long after James joined, in early 2006 there was a series of large profit warnings caused by difficulties with the NPfIT project, which led the shares to crash.

Finally, what many had been waiting years for happened: the announcement that iSoft was going to change its accounting policy for the recognition of revenue from the sale of software. But what a wait! Together with an impairment of the goodwill carried in the balance sheet in respect of the acquisition of Torex in 2004; the adoption of a more appropriate revenue recognition policy; and the movement of off balance sheet financing on to the balance sheet, with associated interest, iSoft reported a loss for 2006 of a staggering £344 million. The previous year, under less conservative accounting for revenue recognition, off balance sheet finance and goodwill, iSoft reported a profit of £44 million. Quite a turnaround and quite a difference in the interpretation of accounting standards, which to many were starting to look like every finance director's flexible friend. Not surprising, then, that the shares had a hard landing. In October 2007 iSoft was bought by IBA Health Ltd of Australia for £156 million – a mere 15% of its value when it was at its stock market peak. Following further takeover activity in the IT sector, iSoft's ultimate owner is now DXC Technology, the enterprise services arm of Hewlett-Packard.

Hard landing

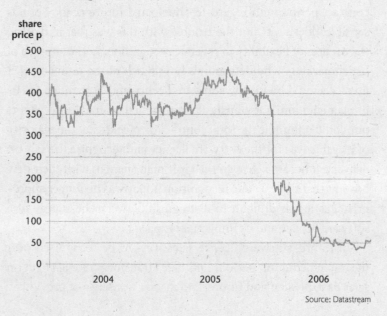

Source: Datastream

What a wait!

iSoft changed its revenue recognition policy in mid 2006. Maybe it was because of the arrival of experienced finance director Gavin James. Perhaps it was because of the severe difficulties it was having with the NHS IT project. Maybe it was just time.

Before 2006, iSoft had recognised sales of both software and installation and service in accordance with US GAAP – in particular SOP97-2, Software Revenue Recognition, and SAB (Staff Accounting Bulletin) 101. This allowed them to unbundle a contract into its various parts: the sale of the software licence; the sale of the implementation; and the sale for service, for example. The sale of the software licence was recognised on delivery; the implementation sale was recognised over the implementation period; and the service sale was recognised over the service contract period with regard to anticipated future costs. Sounds sensible, doesn't it? But the trouble with this was that it allowed a great deal of flexibility in revenue recognition. In the absence of benchmarking, who determines how much of the total contract invoice should be for the software licence and how much for its implementation? Obviously if one wanted to maximise profits one could unbundle the total contract invoice so that the majority of its value was for the software licence and recognise the sale on delivery. It became clear to the iSoft management with their new brooms that this revenue recognition policy was no longer appropriate, as it was difficult to distinguish between the supply of a software licence and its implementation.

In future, software licence sales were to be recognised over the implementation period. This had a transformational effect on sales past, present and future, and made a nonsense of previously reported profit numbers. For example, previously under US GAAP, for 2005 a profit before tax of £44.5 million had been reported on sales of £262 million. Now, under IFRS, the 2005 profit before tax was a mere £2.1 million on sales of £186 million. That's quite a difference, and no wonder bankers, regulators and new shareholders in particular became very agitated.

Revenue moves to the right with consequences

£m	2003	2004	2005	2006	2007	2008	2009	2010	2011	Total
Sales under old US GAAP accounting	44	54	76							174
Sales under new IFRS accounting					45	45	28	28	28	174

Source: iSoft 2006 Annual Report

In addition to the massive revenue recognition adjustments iSoft made in 2006 (shown above), new management also brought on to the balance sheet £62 million of financing and associated interest hitherto hidden from sight. They also impaired the substantial goodwill in the balance sheet in respect of the Torex acquisition, writing it down from £495 million to £144 million. These are big numbers indeed. With all these sizeable adjustments there were inevitable consequences: the company's banking arrangements had to be amended, at very considerable cost; the board, not surprisingly, underwent change; the brouhaha caused clients to be reticent about iSoft's products; an investigation into accounting irregularities was initiated by Deloitte & Touche; and the Financial Services Authority (FSA), the forerunner of today's Financial Conduct Authority (FCA), commenced its own enquiries.

The FSA initiated legal proceedings against four directors and founders of iSoft for misleading investors about the firm's financial position. At the first trial, in 2013, the jury failed to reach a verdict in this complicated accounting case. The second trial, in 2015, ground to a halt on a procedural problem and the FCA abandoned the case and the defendants (who had maintained their innocence) were acquitted. The FRC, the auditors' regulator, judged that the company's auditors, RSM Robson Rhodes, had fallen short of the standard reasonably expected of auditors and ordered them to pay a derisory fine and costs of nearly £1 million. They also banned two of the iSoft accountants from the profession.

A hard landing was inevitable

After the issues at Cedar Group a few years before iSoft blew up, many people were wary of software companies with large amounts of accrued income. Remember, accrued income is often an estimate and, in the case of a software company, can be almost pure profit. Until it changed its revenue recognition policy, the accounts of iSoft were loaded up with levels of accrued income that many thought incredible but which were none the less signed off by the auditors.

The 2004 iSoft Annual Report was the one on which questions about the amount of accrued income should first have been raised, but the 2005 iSoft Annual Report was a palpable example of excessive accrued income, too.

The extract from **Note 16 – Debtors** (see next page) tells us many things that would worry anyone with a bit of accounting knowledge: there were large amounts of accrued income; iSoft appeared to be waiting a very long time for its money, which was

Note 16: Debtors, an extract, £'000

	Group 2005	Company 2005	Group 2004	Company 2004
Trade debtors	57,565	–	42,380	–
Amounts owed by Group undertakings	–	100,001	–	113,980
Amounts recoverable on contracts	19,495		–	–
Deferred taxation	2,947	–	9,513	–
Other debtors	4,478	457	4,938	463
Prepayments and accrued income	33,220	172	50,105	145
	117,705	100,630	106,936	114,588

Prepayments and accrued income include a balance of **£6,887,000** (2004: **£4,215,000**) due after one year.

Source: 2005 iSoft Annual Report

Means iSoft waits 153 days on average to be paid

Means iSoft waits 225 days on average to be paid

not good for its cash flow – in 2004 its average wait was 225 days, meaning some clients may have taken twice that time to pay; iSoft only expected to be paid for some of the accrued income in over a year's time; and for 2005 there is the sudden appearance of another subjective balance for amounts recoverable on contracts of £19.5 million, with no comparative number for 2004. There were plenty of warning signs in this note to the accounts that showed that cash flow was totally out of step with reported revenues, which suggested that the latter were likely to have been overstated.

Lesson

The lesson is that you should learn from the experiences of other companies in similar businesses. The 2000 Cedar Group Annual Report (see page 67) was overloaded with large accrued income balances – and that company had gone bust six years earlier, pretty much in the middle of a rights issue to raise desperately needed funds. Both Cedar and iSoft operated in the same industry and had accounts with similar characteristics – there should have been a feeling of déjà vu. In 2004, iSoft had an accrued income balance even larger than its trade debtors. In other words, it said it was owed more from its subjective accrual of income than from clients it had actually invoiced. Knowing that sales of software are nearly all profit, one has to be very wary of IT companies that accrue large amounts of income.

Utilitywise

SHOCKING!

The flashing warning lights were there for both wise and unwise investors to see. But the unwise did not look. The 2013 Utilitywise Annual Report, published following the company's successful listing on AIM, had plenty in it to become energised about. Seemingly few cared as, a year after flotation, the company's shares had powered their way to three times what they had been worth at the IPO. This inflated share price did not last long when some were shocked to discover that the company's revenue recognition policy allowed large amounts of accrued income to be reported.

Utilitywise is a third party intermediary (TPI) and sometimes referred to as an energy broker. TPIs help their clients – which are predominantly companies, both large and small – get the best deal for their power requirements, mostly gas and electricity, and they make their money from the commission paid directly to them by the energy provider. There are suggestions that some TPIs are conflicted as they promote certain energy providers over others, in favour of those that pay the most commission, but there is no suggestion that Utilitywise did this. Utilitywise had a broad range of customers, from single-site clients to those with large multi-site activities. The company planned to capitalise on its position in the energy market by offering energy management products and services such as smart metering, energy audits and other items to manage and monitor clients' energy consumption.

Utilitywise felt that the fragmented UK energy market was ripe for consolidation and, because of the low penetration of TPIs, it would be able to increase its market share both through the growth of its own business and by acquisition. From 2009 to 2014 the UK energy market had seen rising prices, and it was believed that commercial customers would seek out TPIs such as Utilitywise to help mitigate their increasing energy costs. Great strategy idea, but in practice things panned out differently because Utilitywise was aggressive in estimating the levels of commissions payable from energy providers, and it was also aggressive in the timing of its recognition of this revenue. IAS 18 – Revenue, the accounting standard which it employed here, helped it to do this as it allowed the company to take commissions as accrued income in the income statement well ahead of the arrival of the cash itself – indeed, as soon as the client had signed the supply contract.

Plenty of shocks

Within a year of the IPO in 2012, the Utilitywise share price was firmly on a downward trajectory as eyebrows began to be raised over the extent of the growing accrued income balances. There was also a great deal of bad news that subsequently helped the share price on its way down. Let me list a few of the shocks that hastened the downward impetus:

- A profit warning was announced in 2015 because of increased expenditure on infrastructure.

- The company employed a greater number of sales consultants to push for more energy contracts and therefore costs were higher than originally expected.

- In early 2017, Utilitywise said that it would no longer take upfront cash payments for commissions from energy suppliers because sometimes the energy consumption by clients did not meet expectations. This clearly had negative cash flow implications.

- Later in 2017, Utiltywise announced that there had been under-consumption in a number of contracts on which it had already received commissions. This meant the company was going to have to repay these unearned commissions back to the energy provider.

- Also later in 2017, Utilitywise said that it would early adopt IFRS 15 – Revenue from Contracts with Customers for revenue recognition. This much more conservative way of recognising revenue than had been previously adopted would cause reported profits to be significantly reduced. IFRS 15 ensures that revenues in the future are recognised more in line with when cash is received. The company also announced that much more conservative estimates of expected revenues from clients would be recognised and that the final dividend would not be paid, as the balance sheet was now expected to show no net assets, only net liabilities.

- Because of the complexity of applying IFRS 15 and the work required to establish the more conservative amounts of commission it recognised as income, Utilitywise's auditors requested help from … another set of auditors! If investors had not already lost faith in Utilitywise, they soon would do.

- Many of the directors resigned during this difficult period.
- The shares were suspended in January 2018.
- The publication of the company's results for 2017 were delayed until eight months after the July 2017 year end. Whilst the announcement commenced with 'Operational Highlights', these were irrelevant when compared to the lowlights of the reported £31 million of losses and a balance sheet which showed net liabilities of £16 million.
- There were some who saw Utilitywise as an income stock, comparing it to a utility, but dividends were definitely now a pipe dream.

The 2017 Utilitywise Annual Report also restated the 2016 results on the basis of more conservative revenue recognition. This included some big changes to numbers some had previously relied on. Sales that were originally reported as £84 million were now restated as £68 million; profits that were originally stated at £18 million were now restated at £2 million; and the balance sheet that was originally reported as having £59 million of net assets now had only £16 million of net assets. Quite different then.

Hazard lights clearly visible

The warning signs that there may be trouble ahead were well illuminated in the 2013 Utilitywise Annual Report, and indeed in subsequent ones. New management set the record straighter in early 2018 when it finally reported nearly eight months after

A shocking share price fall

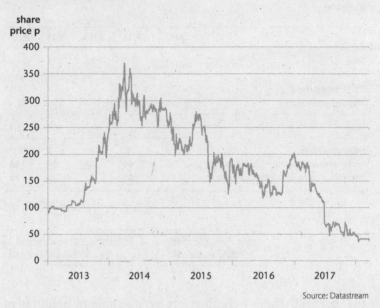

Source: Datastream

the year end (quoted companies are normally required to publish their results within four months of their year end).

Large amounts of accrued income are usually a sign of bad things to come, but it is always a surprise that it takes so long for corrective action to be taken by those who are meant to know best. The light shone by new management showed the full picture as the accounts were finally adjusted and a more conservative approach to the amounts of revenue recognised was adopted.

The analysis on the next page shows that in all the years that Utilitywise was a public company, over half of the reported sales in the income statement for any one year were unpaid by clients (in this case, a small number of well-known energy suppliers) at

Analysis of sales, trade receivables, accrued and deferred income, £m

	2012	2013	2014	2015	2016
Sales	14.4	25.3	49.0	69.1	84.4
Trade receivables	0.8	3.8	4.1	5.9	6.5
Accrued income	1.5	11.4	22.2	31.5	40.4
Total	2.3	15.2	26.3	37.4	46.9
Deferred income	1.3	7.2	10.4	7.9	11.5
Receivables and accrued income as % of sales	16	60	54	54	56
Deferred income as % of accrued income	86	63	47	25	28

Source: 2012, 2013, 2014, 2015, 2016 Utilitywise Annual Reports

More than 50% of sales unpaid at year end	Significant decline in deferred income as a % of accrued income

the year end. There were therefore very significant amounts of accrued income. In the original accounts for 2016, the final year before the massive adjustments, accrued income made up very nearly 50% of sales. During the period up to 2016 there was a significant decline in deferred income expressed as a percentage of accrued income. So there was plenty in the accounts to cause eyebrows to be raised, but by 2016 the damage was already done to the share price and most investors had lost money.

There was yet another telltale warning sign in the 2013 Utilitywise Annual Report that could have saved investors millions if they had understood its significance. It showed that there had been a subtle but material change to the way commission income was accounted for at the company.

Let me explain. Utilitywise determined its accrued revenues by establishing the present value of expected cash flows of commissions from energy suppliers. These expected cash flows and present values were determined by the past payment experience of clients recorded by Utilitywise in its database, with adjustments being made to allow for some under-consumption by users and therefore reduced commissions being payable. But these adjustments were subsequently found to be far too optimistic and were the main reason Utilitywise had to reformulate its accounts for 2016 and 2017.

In order to calculate the present value of expected cash flows to be received as commissions from energy suppliers, a discount rate must be employed to adjust for the time value of money. Cash now and in the hand is worth more than cash received in, say, one year's time. This discount rate usually equates to the cost of capital of the company – the cost of capital is the cost of funds used to finance the company's activities and is usually made up of the cost of debt and the cost of equity. In 2013, Utilitywise chose to reduce its discount rate from 9% to 3%, on the basis that the new rate more accurately reflected the risk of trading with blue chip energy companies – see **Note 1 Accounting Policies: Prior period adjustment** (next page). This is very significant – not only is 3% a very low discount rate but also its use substantially increases the present value of revenues and with it Utilitywise's profits. What Utilitywise omitted to mention at the time was that, while the energy companies were regarded as blue chip (although there are some who might reasonably question that), their clients certainly were not and it was they who consumed the power for which Utilitywise got paid its commission.

Some would say that the provisions made (a 15% deduction to expected commissions) for some under-consumption by clients

Note 1: Accounting policies: Prior period adjustment, an extract

During the preparation of the current year financial statements management has considered the discount rate applied to the expected future cash flows from revenue. After due consideration management now believe that the discount rate of **9%** previously applied was a misstatement and did not appropriately reflect the risk associated with this revenue. The discounting rate has therefore been revised to **3%** to more accurately reflect the risk of trading with blue-chip energy companies.

Source: 2013 Utilitywise Annual Report

> *Reduction in the discount rate applied to future cash flows*

went some way to account for this new lower discount rate, slicing the previous discount rate by two-thirds in just one year was worthy of explanation. Utilitywise now conservatively provides for an under-consumption rate of between 25% and 30% – quite a difference from the 15% of previous years.

Reducing the discount rate used to calculate the present value of a stream of cash flows from 9% to 3% has a very material effect. £10,000 might be a typical annual commission that Utilitywise received from a utility company in respect of a client. This amount received each year for three years (the length of a typical energy supply contract period) discounted at 3% is worth 12% more than those same cash flows discounted at 9%. This increase is pure profit. So by reducing the discount rate for expected commissions, revenues were significantly increased at Utilitywise and were all taken upfront through the income statement ahead of when the cash was actually received.

In contrast to the new reduced discount rate of 3% employed by Utilitywise to establish its revenues, and hence its profits, the company chose to use the much higher discount rates of 9%,

Effect of changing the discount rate on present value and hence revenues, £

Annual commission on a contract	Contract period	Discount rate	Present value
10,000	3 years	9%	**25,000**
10,000	3 years	3%	**28,000**
10,000	5 years	9%	**39,000**
10,000	5 years	3%	**46,000**

Reducing the discount rate from 9% to 3% boosts revenues by 12% for 3 year contracts	*Reducing the discount rate from 9% to 3% boosts revenues by 18% for 5 year contracts*

16% and 18% to justify the goodwill amounts in its balance sheet for the various acquisitions it made. This is shown in Note 13 – Goodwill in the 2013 Utilitywise Annual Report (too large a note to show here). How can it be that some of the same cash flows are discounted at different rates in order to determine revenues for the income statement, on the one hand, and goodwill for the balance sheet on the other?

Lesson

Quite apart from the ludicrously large amounts of accrued income, which should always raise questions about revenue recognition, the dramatic reduction seen to the discount rate employed in 2013 to value Utilitywise's commissions receivable from its energy suppliers was a warning that its accounts were of limited value to investors. The hazard lights were flashing and were bright.

One is also entitled to ask why the 3% discount rate employed to value Utilitywise's revenues was so very different from the discount rates of 9%, 16% and 18% used to justify the goodwill balances. The cash flows are, after all, the same ones. There is some mitigation here in that an under-consumption provision was employed, but it was not big enough. It certainly did not mitigate enough when under-consumption on energy contracts was estimated at 15%. Some large contracts at Utilitywise under-consumed by as much as 50%.

Utilitywise has now chosen to adopt IFRS 15 – Revenue for Contracts with Customers early, which will reduce the large accrued income amounts further and align profits more with cash. This is a welcome move in the right direction as Utilitywise and its new management commences the company's rehabilitation.

Slater and Gordon – and Quindell

AMBULANCE CHASER IN CAR CRASH

You would have thought that a company full of ambulance chasers would be able to avoid a car crash when they saw one. But not this Australian firm of lawyers, it would appear. Slater and Gordon, which specialises in personal injury and was the first legal firm in the world to be listed on a stock exchange, saw its share price collapse in 2015 as investors realised that its acquisition-led expansion had been done without adequate due diligence – surely something that should come as second nature to a company full of lawyers?

Slater and Gordon has an illustrious history. Established in 1935, it employed Julia Gillard before she entered politics and went on to become Australia's first woman prime minister. The roll call of high-profile cases it has been involved in include: asbestosis claims at the Wittenoom mine in Western Australia and environmental claims for the local inhabitants of Papua New Guinea against BHP, one of the world's biggest mining companies. It has also acted for Vietnam War conscientious objectors, Thalidomide victims in Australia and New Zealand, and those with claims for faulty breast implants. Quite a testimony to its past glories indeed.

Slater and Gordon floated on the Australian Stock Exchange in 2007 at A$1 and, as the UK's legal market was four to five times larger than Australia's, the company embarked on a strategy of making acquisitions there. In 2012 it acquired Russell Jones & Walker for £53.8 million. More UK acquisitions followed, aided by the access to cash that the listing of shares on a stock exchange afforded. Its largest acquisition by far was the personal injury business of the controversial UK quoted company Quindell, which it bought for a whopping £637 million (A$1300 million) in 2015. Those unfortunate shareholders who applied for shares at A$6.37 for the privilege of assisting Slater and Gordon in its purchase will not be getting much return on their money. As a result of its acquisitions, Slater and Gordon ended up with more employees in the UK than in Australia – and the firm became famous for its effective hard-sell TV adverts offering a no-win, no-fee compensation claim service. Whiplash injuries caused by car accidents were a speciality. The company's advertising strap line was 'Your case is our cause'.

Slater and Gordon is now a mere shadow of its former self because of its over-ambitious expansion plan in the UK, proving that people businesses such as lawyers, accountants, architects and stockbrokers are often better off as partnerships as their assets go up and down in the lifts every day and can quite as easily walk out of the door. Slater and Gordon shares are almost worthless now and the owners of the company's debt are in the driving seat following the crash in its share price. The UK activities so carelessly acquired by Slater and Gordon have now been demerged from its Australian activities and are run for the benefit of the hedge funds who own the debt in that business.

Share price collapses after acquisition from Quindell

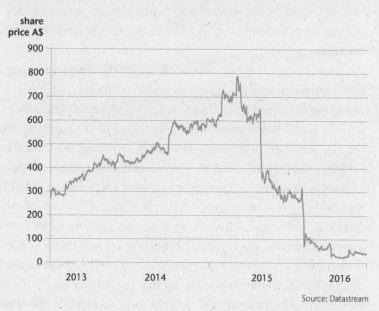

Source: Datastream

From A$2.2 billion to nothing

Almost immediately after its acquisition of Quindell's personal injury business in May 2015, the shares of Slater and Gordon started their downward spiral to becoming virtually worthless. Ahead of the acquisition, Slater and Gordon apparently reviewed over 8000 case files using seventy of its own lawyers to do the work. They even took independent advice from external advisers to ensure that the Quindell personal injury business was correctly valued. Neither the internal nor the external teams found anything untoward in their due diligence, so the acquisition went ahead. But even if they had not looked at the books at Quindell, surely they had read the papers? Or they could have watched *Quindell – The Official Downfall Movie* on YouTube, which likened Adolf Hitler's last days in his bunker with Quindell management's attempts to keep the company's share price from crashing.

Shortly after the acquisition of Quindell's personal injury activities, the Australian Securities and Investments Commission raised queries about Slater and Gordon's own accounting procedures. Consolidation errors were also found in the reporting of the UK activities. Less than a year after acquiring the Quindell business, Slater and Gordon realised it had made a terrible mistake and wrote down its UK investment by over £400 million (A$814 million). One can only assume it was the qualification of the 2014 Quindell Annual Report on 5 August 2015 by KPMG, the announcement by the Financial Reporting Council that it was to undertake an enquiry into Quindell's accounting on the same day, and the announcement also that day that the Serious Fraud Office was opening a criminal case into the business and accounting practices of Quindell that shook them out of their due diligence complacency. It was quite a day for both Quindell and Slater and Gordon. Slater and Gordon ultimately reported a loss of over £500 million (A$1017 million) in 2016, mainly as a result of the write-down in the value of the business it had acquired from Quindell. So much for all that due diligence.

Slater and Gordon had not been conservative in the way it recognised revenues. It had recognised revenue for its Australian no-win, no-fee work under Australian Accounting Standards Board (AASB) 118, whereby revenue was recognised when it was 'probable' that economic benefits would flow to the company. It was now decided it needed to apply AASB 15, which meant that revenue could be recognised only when it was 'highly probable that a significant reversal of revenue recognised will not occur'. The new policy was much more conservative than before and avoided an over-reliance on management judgement, which had tended to be too optimistic. The standards applied in Australia were a lot less rigorous than those that should have been applied in the UK. It seems that, as regards personal injury claims, there was a wide disparity between revenue recognition policies from one end of the world to the other. Perhaps that is why the seventy internal lawyers at Slater and Gordon who did the due diligence work on Quindell waved the acquisition through.

It will be no shock to anyone that the board of directors at Slater and Gordon has changed. The debt of A$780 million has been restated to a significantly reduced A$30 million in exchange for 95% of the equity of the Australian business passing to the debt holders. The UK activities have been demerged. There has been a shareholder settlement of A$36 million paid – an admission that the Quindell acquisition had been a disaster of a due diligence exercise. Slater and Gordon have filed a claim against Quindell (now called Watchstone Group) for £600 million. Oh, and there was a further write-down of the UK business in 2017 as goodwill on it was impaired by a further A$350 million. Slater and Gordon, having paid A$1300 million for Quindell's personal injury business in May 2015, was now saying it was just about worthless. At its peak in 2015 after the placing of shares to finance the ill-fated Quindell personal injury acquisition, Slater and Gordon's market value was A$2.2 billion. At the end of 2017 it was just A$17 million. But all of this loss could have been avoided – if only the due diligence lawyers had read the 2013 Quindell Annual Report and understood it.

Big accruals stretching the rules

Note 21 – Trade and other receivables (below) in the 2013 Quindell Annual Report tells us that there was a great deal of subjectivity in its revenue recognition. The accrued income included in the annual report accounted for a massive 40% of sales. The accrued income amount was also much bigger than the trade receivables by quite some margin – a major warning sign that revenue recognition may not have been as conservative as it should be. Remember that accrued income is un-invoiced revenue and so it is a difficult

Note 21: Trade and other receivables, £'000

	2013	2012
Trade receivables (net of impairment provision)	85,632	73,694
Other receivables:		
relating to legal disbursements due from insurance companies	57,473	26,549
other	20,120	7,977
Prepayments	12,955	8,426
Accrued income	**151,693**	47,928
Derivative financial instruments	–	13,297
	327,873	177,871

Source: 2013 Quindell Annual Report

Included above within gross trade receivables (ie excluding impairment provisions) due from third parties is **£91,270,000** (2012: £70,487,000) relating to debts over which security (by way of fixed and floating charges) has been taken as part of the provision of invoice discounting facilities to companies in the Group, further details of which are provided in note 24. The directors consider that the net carrying amount of trade receivables approximates to their fair value.

Trade receivables used to secure borrowings through invoice discounting	Very large accrued income accounting for 40% of Quindell sales

number for the auditors to substantiate. Adjusting for disbursements, Quindell appeared to be waiting between seven and eight months for its money. By contrast – and this is the telling part – in 2015, the year it acquired Quindell, Slater and Gordon was waiting five to six months for its money. This discrepancy between two similar firms doing the same kind of legal work should have been subject to rigorous due diligence. One other point – Quindell was borrowing on the security of its receivable book before taking account of the bad debt provision. Note 21 tells us that Quindell was borrowing more on the security of receivables than it thought the receivables were actually worth. Who lends on that basis?

For 2013, Quindell originally reported a profit after tax of £83 million. After adjusting mainly for the revenue recognition issues, so plainly displayed to any reader with a smattering of accounting knowledge in its 2013 annual report and outlined above, the company restated its 2013 performance to a loss of £68 million in August 2015. Quite a difference, really, and one that Slater and Gordon will point to as they pursue Watchstone Group for the £600 million they still think they are owed.

Lesson

Be wary of large accruals of income. Large accruals of income are an obvious warning sign that there may be revenue recognition issues. These were clear at Quindell and they should have been picked up in a rigorous due diligence process. In the 2013 Quindell Annual Report the accrued income figure was so large when compared to the previous year's – and indeed to all the other figures included in current assets and current liabilities – that a thorough justification was required. The car crash was inevitable. A case of no win, big loss for investors in Slater and Gordon.

Redcentric

DÉJÀ VU

Whenever I read about Redcentric I have a feeling of déjà vu. It is just like many of the IT companies whose share prices dived in the period from 2000 and the Millennium Bug anti-climax to 2010. These included Cedar Group, which had the rare accolade of suffering from a failed rights issue and was a company like many in the sector that overstated its revenue before it collapsed, and Guardian IT, a disaster recovery company that was a disaster itself. Redcentric at the time was in many ways a combination of these two as it had similar activities to both Cedar Group and Guardian IT.

As we should always remember, history repeats itself, especially in the types of company disasters and more especially with IT companies. Perhaps it is unfair to say that Redcentric was a disaster like others in the UK IT world. It survives today under new management, but the share price dived in 2015 and many investors must be in the red today. Redcentric is an IT service company, which helps clients like Evans Cycles and Howden Joinery redesign their IT systems and manages them, often using the cloud to host data and software. It is a young company,

Red faces at Redcentric

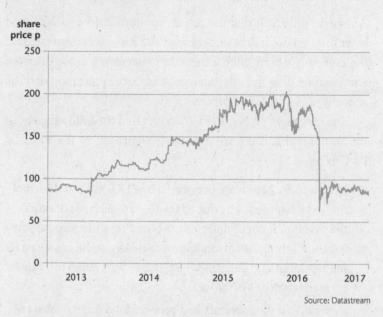

share price p

Source: Datastream

established in 2013 but now has over 2000 mid-tier clients, many of whom receive services from Redcentric delivered from its data centres in Reading, Harrogate, Cambridge and London.

So far so good and credit to them for managing the critical IT systems of such a large number of clients. By the look of the share price graph above, it was all going rather well for a while before the board announced that it had commenced a review of the company's accounts, indicating that assets looked to have been overstated by at least £10 million and that net debt had been understated in the past. Reason enough for the share price to dive vertically, which it duly did. The finance director was put on gardening leave.

All is forensically revealed

A review confirmed that the results for both 2015 and 2016 had been flattered, with debt understated and net assets overstated. In the company's own words, these 'misstatements arose due to a combination of wilful misstatement and poor application of basic accounting controls and processes'.

The investigation begun in 2016 revealed the following about the accounts that had been previously signed off by the auditors, PwC in Leeds.

■ Net assets in 2016 were overstated by £15.8 million. Much of this overstatement was due to inadequate accruals of costs, the overstatement of deferred costs and revenue recognition issues. All things where judgements needed to be exercised by management and perhaps where the auditor relied too much on management assurances.

■ It seems that the accounts had been misstated for at least two years – in 2015 as well as 2016.

■ Net debt in 2016 was understated by £12.5 million. Apparently, payments from clients received after the year end were included as received before the year end, with the effect that they were recorded either as cash or a reduction in debt.

■ Cash payments to suppliers paid before the year end were incorrectly recorded as paid after the year end and therefore not deducted from cash. Bank reconciliations by the auditors should have revealed this. Getting a company's cash balance so wrong is careless at best.

■ Payments to suppliers in 2015 and 2016 had been delayed to keep debt down.

■ The original 2016 income statement reported a profit of £7.4 million. Once the investigators from Deloitte and Nabarro had done their work, the profit turned into a loss of £6.1 million. Quite a difference.

As a result of the investigation, both the chief executive and the finance director left the company, and in March 2017, the FCA announced its own investigation into Redcentric's publication of accounting information and other statements it had made concerning its financial position. In February 2017 and July 2017, the FRC announced that they were investigating the audit and also the preparation of the financial statements of Redcentric respectively.

Red flags

A quick and easy way of spotting possible accounting shenanigans is to take two fingers and run them down the current and comparative year numbers in the annual report. But first, make a mental note of the company's activity level change in the year. A good proxy for this is the change in level of sales in the period. In my opinion it is fine if other numbers in the annual report change from one year to the other by the change in activity levels. If the change in current year numbers differ significantly from the change in activity levels shown by the sales change, management should be asked to explain the reason for the disparity. At Redcentric there were a number of key numbers, where management estimates and judgement were required, that looked way out relative to activity levels. Given that reported sales in 2016 rose by only 16%, the following large increases looked odd – see **Consolidated Income Statement, year ended 31 March** (next page).

Consolidated Income Statement, year ended 31 March, an extract, £'000

	2016	2015
Revenue	109,526	94,321
Cost of sales	(45,050)	(40,596)
Gross profit	64,476	53,725
Selling and distribution costs	(8,688)	(9,285)
Administrative expenses	(47,349)	(35,770)
Adjusted EBITDA	25,844	21,403

Source: 2016 Redcentric Annual Report

Only a 16% increase in activity levels

Note 12: Trade and other receivables, an extract, £'000

	2016	2015
Trade receivables	21,693	10,208
Less: provision for impairment of trade receivables	(661)	(76)
Trade receivables – net	21,032	10,132
Other receivables	8	25
Prepayments	5,777	2,833
Accrued income	8,945	5,360
	35,762	18,350

Source: 2016 Redcentric Annual Report

As at 31 March, trade receivables of **£6.2m (2015: £1.3m)** were past due but not impaired.

107% increase in trade receivables

104% increase in prepayments

376% increase in trade receivables past due but not impaired

66% increase in accrued income

- Trade receivables rose by 107% – see **Note 12: Trade and other receivables.**
- Prepayments rose by 104% – see **Note 12.**
- Accrued income rose by 66% – see **Note 12.**
- Trade receivables past due but not impaired rose by 376% – see **Note 12.**
- Trade payables rose by 60% – see **Note 14: Trade and other payables.**

The first four of these unusually large increases boost profits substantially and could indicate aggressive revenue recognition and the deferral of costs. The fifth is also helpful in that by taking longer to pay suppliers, the cash position looks better than if they had been paid on time. In the case of Redcentric which had no net cash, by paying suppliers late reported debt was lower than it might have otherwise been. Such window dressing may have helped Redcentric avoid breaching banking covenants.

Note 14: Trade and other payables, an extract, £'000

	2016	2015
Trade payables	12,126	7,582
Other payables	971	111
Taxation and social security	4,866	3,063
Accruals	3,959	3,871
Deferred income	4,648	3,915
	26,570	18,542

Source: 2016 Redcentric Annual Report

60% increase in trade payables

Called to account

The auditor, PwC in Leeds, was fined £4.6 million and the two partners that undertook the audit were fined £140,000 each. The FRC levied the fines because it believed that the auditors had failed to apply sufficient professional scepticism. Perhaps because the Leeds office of PwC was also the auditor to the failed retailer BHS, the FRC instructed PwC to supplement its ongoing monitoring and support for that office in order to improve the quality of its audit. Presumably this means that staff at PwC in Leeds, including in particular the two partners involved in the audit of Redcentric, were required to be retrained. Not surprising really that the FRC took such action: the understatement of debt would have been an easy spot for any competent auditor, as bank reconciliations are what all trainee auditors master early on in their professional lives.

Lesson

For those aware of the troubles that hit Cedar Group in 2000 and Guardian IT in 2001, and indeed other IT company disasters in later years, the Redcentric share collapse should have been no surprise at all. The 2016 Redcentric Annual Report contained enough red warning flags that the company was heading for a fall. The numbers just did not stack up. Balance sheet items, some of which reflected what was allegedly owed to the company by clients, did not sit comfortably with the far more pedestrian growth in sales. Redcentric was also taking far too long to pay its suppliers, which means that at the year-end, debt was manipulated to be lower than it really should have been.

PART 4

Not so good

WHEN GOODWILL GOES BAD

Goodwill is an intangible asset, recorded as such in a company's balance sheet. Under IFRS 3 – Business Combinations, it is the difference between what a company pays for another company and the assets acquired with that acquisition. Under IAS 36 – Impairment of Assets, the goodwill on the balance sheet should be tested for impairment annually so that its value can be justified. Often goodwill is a big number, especially if a company has been very acquisitive. The main thing about IAS 36 is that the goodwill must not be carried in the balance sheet at more than the amount that can be recovered from its use or sale – the recoverable amount. If the carrying value in the balance sheet is more than the recoverable amount, it is said to be 'impaired', and this difference must be recognised as a loss in the income statement. The recoverable amount is the higher of the fair value less costs of disposal and the value in use. If there is no market for the goodwill asset and it cannot be sold, the value in use is calculated by determining future cash flows and discounting them at an appropriate rate in order to arrive at a present value of those cash flows. This requires the auditors to satisfy themselves that the cash projections of each cash generating unit (CGU) are reasonable and justified.

The outsourcing company Mitie has reported large losses in recent years, but it survives through the efforts of new and improved management. In 2017, the loss reported was £183 million, which was mainly the result of writing down the goodwill on its health-care division, MiHomecare, when Mitie sold it for just £2. But only in 2016 the firm's auditors signed off that they believed the recoverable amount for this business was £145 million, thereby justifying its carrying value in the 2016 Mitie Annual Report of £107 million. So in only ten months, MiHomecare went from being worth £107 million in Mitie's balance sheet to no more than the price of a National Lottery ticket. Incredibly, Mitie's auditors had apparently been happy to accept as reasonable that MiHomecare would grow by 16% in a year, even though sales had declined by 15% in the previous year, and that, even though losses were posted in that period, the business would be profitable in the future despite pressures such as the minimum wage. This was simply not credible, so the auditor must have relied on management assurances as to MiHomecare's future projects without reference to its past trading performance.

Mitie

WHAT A WAIT

Mitie look after buildings inside and out – they call it facilities management. So if you need catering, security, cleaning or maintenance for your building, then Mitie would be a company to call. In the early days these jobs were delivered to clients as discrete single services. Then services were bundled up, so that perhaps both cleaning and maintenance were supplied, which often meant that the client saved money. The next step was integrated services, whereby Mitie would be trusted to provide all the services to keep a building functioning, in return for further cost savings to the client. Integrated service contracts tended to be longer term and embedded in the client's activities. The number and size of integrated service contracts was an important key performance indicator (KPI) for investors. Lloyds Bank, Sky, Rolls-Royce and, funnily enough, Deloitte, the company's auditors back in the day, would become important clients for Mitie.

Mitie used to take stakes in smaller facilities management companies and offer to buy out the founders completely if certain targets were met – Mitie stands for Management Incentive Through Investment in Equity – but this old model was gradually phased out in favour of outright acquisition. In 2012 Mitie bought Enara, a home care specialist, for £111 million in cash and another care company, Complete Care, for £9 million. Mitie amalgamated these businesses providing services to infirm people in their own homes and renamed them MiHomecare, but in 2017 they sold it for just £2 and even had to pay the buyers £9.5 million to clinch the deal, putting the loss on disposal of MiHomecare at over £132 million. This disastrous mistake prompted the departure of the old management and large adjustments to Mitie's past accounts.

In 2017, Mitie reported losses of £183 million – much of which related to the disposal of MiHomecare and accounting adjustments that reflected the more conservative approach of newly appointed management. Mitie also restated its results for 2015 and 2016 – not something one expects to see from a FTSE 250 company with a blue chip auditor, even though most in the City were not in the least surprised. The new management got straight to work and, with investigating accountants KPMG, confirmed what many had suspected for a long time: Mitie's historic profits had been materially overstated. How come it had taken so long for the truth to come out?

The new management in charge of Mitie hope that they will turn the company round, in particular through the use of increased levels of technology that can harness all the data available about a building. They call this the 'connected workplace' and have high hopes that this change will be welcomed by those who need sophisticated property managed for them. A change at Mitie had been long overdue.

A series of profit warnings

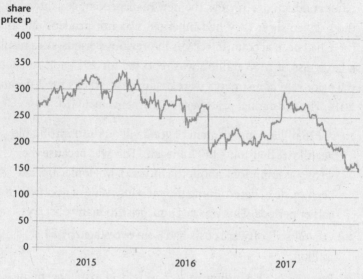

share price p

Source: Datastream

The City saw the warning signs

There were very few significant UK shareholders in Mitie in 2016, when the company's shares commenced their fall. No one rated the old management – or its methods of accounting, for that matter. The significant shareholders were mostly US investors who perhaps had not read the accounts. After a series of three profit warnings in four months in 2016 and early 2017, it was clearly time for a change and management paid the price, with the chief executive, Baroness Ruby McGregor-Smith, and the finance director, Suzanne Baxter, leaving quickly.

An accounting review

After conducting a review, the new management concluded that the balance sheet they had inherited was not prudent and that there had been accounting errors in previous periods. As a result, a large loss of £183 million was reported for 2017 and substantial prior year adjustments were made to the results for 2015 and 2016. The substantial prior year adjustments included:

- A £26 million impairment of goodwill on the unprofitable healthcare division – MiHomecare. This was because the wrong assumptions about the future of MiHomecare had been made in determining the carrying value of goodwill in earlier periods. This was not a surprise to many observers.

- Capitalised software costs had been overstated by £2.8 million.

- Bonuses of £8.3 million, which were paid to management in the year ended March 2017, should have been recorded in 2015 and 2016, as this was the period they related to. You may wonder why bonuses were paid at all.

- Further contract provisions and insurance claims of £8.1 million were made in respect of previous years.

- The way that revenue had previously been recognised meant that trade receivables and accrued income had been overstated by £20.4 million.

- In total, the prior year adjustments amounted to a £66 million pre-tax reduction in profits for 2015 and 2016 – a 48% reduction on previously reported profits for those two years. Where were all the checks and balances usually expected of a large publicly quoted company in 2015 and 2016?

The loss of £183 million reported by Mitie for 2017 was largely due to the £132 million loss on the disposal of MiHomecare and its trading losses, together with a number of one-off items. These included:

- Another £3 million of capitalised software costs being written off.

- The life of software being reduced so that there was an additional amortisation charge of £7 million.

- Accrued income on long-term contracts being reduced by £20 million.

- Further accrued income being reduced, and increased provisions on amounts held as current assets being made of £36 million.

- Impairment of mobilisation costs and other provisions totalling £21 million. Mitie had capitalised costs that were incurred prior to the start of some contracts, which the new management now felt were not recoverable at all.

- All of these one-off items presented the 2017 Mitie Annual Report in a more conservative and prudent way, amounting to adjustments of £88 million in addition to the £132 million loss on the disposal of MiHomecare.

These adjustments are very large and one has to ask whatever convinced the previous auditors to allow the original pre-adjustment figures to stand uncorrected.

All the classic warning signs

The 2015 and 2016 Mitie Annual Reports displayed typical warning signs that all was not well long before the company announced the series of profit warnings that caused the share price to fall – and well before Mitie started assisting the FCA (which has now ceased its investigation into the timing of a 2016 profit warning) and the FRC with their enquiries.

The warning signs included:

- The income statement identified a 'Headline' or 'Before Other Items' performance, so that the large costs of the continual restructuring of the group and its loss-making acquisitions were disclosed separately as if these were unimportant and not part of the ongoing activities of the group at all. They clearly were part of the ongoing activities, as every year there were 'Other Items' and they were significant. 'Other Items' accounted for 40% of profits 'Before Other Items' between 2014 and 2016.

- There were large and rising amounts of accrued income on the balance sheet. In 2016 the accrued income balance (an estimate of what Mitie thought it was owed) of £236 million was even larger than the trade receivable balance of £210 million (the amount that Mitie had invoiced its clients for but which was unpaid at the year end). There is of course nothing wrong with accruing income, but when the balance grows by 30% in a year in which sales fall, it's worth wondering how this could possibly be.

- Mobilisation costs were significant – these were the costs incurred by Mitie after it had been appointed as the preferred bidder on a contract but before it had started – and were capitalised and therefore not recorded as a deduction from profits. In the balance sheet at the end of 2016, £29 million of these costs had been capitalised. This is a large number – so one is entitled to enquire whether some of these costs should have been expensed in the income statement and reduced profits.

- Capitalised software and development costs were rising. There was £44 million of software costs capitalised at the end of 2016. This is another large number also worthy of questioning.

But the largest number in the 2016 Mitie Annual Report that looked plain wrong was the carrying value of goodwill for its healthcare division, MiHomecare. Let me explain. In 2016 Mitie reported the carrying value of goodwill in respect of MiHomecare at £107 million. An extract from the 2016 Mitie Annual Report is shown later.

Goodwill arises in a balance sheet following an acquisition and, as previously explained, it is simply the difference between what one pays for a company and the net assets of the business acquired, and it should be accounted for under IFRS 3 – Business Combinations. Every year this goodwill balance needs to be tested for impairment in accordance with IAS 36 – Impairment of Assets. This is done by preparing a forecast for the acquired business and valuing the expected cash flows by an appropriate discount rate. A number of assumptions need to be made, therefore, which include the expected growth rates of the business, its expected profits and the discount rate used to arrive at a present value for the expected cash flows. The resultant present value is called the 'recoverable amount' and, in this case, should have been more than the goodwill attributed to MiHomecare in the Mitie balance sheet. Of course, the assumptions employed by Mitie in 2016 meant that the goodwill in the balance sheet was easily justified. But the

Note 4: Business and geographical segments, an extract, £m

The group manages its business on a service division basis. These divisions are the basis on which the group reports its primary segmental information.

Business segments – structure during 2016

	Revenue	Operating profit before other items	Operating profit margin before other items	Profit before tax
Soft FM	1,255.1	85.4	6.8%	87.5
Hard FM	618.4	31.7	5.1%	18.5
Property management	280.4	15.8	5.6%	15.8
Healthcare	**78.0**	(4.0)	(5.1%)	**(8.6)**
Other items	–	–	–	(16.4)
Total	2,231.9	128.9	5.8%	96.8

Source: 2016 Mitie Annual Report

Sales at healthcare division fell from £91m in 2015 to £78m in 2016 – a 15% reduction

Losses at healthcare division in 2016

assumptions for the future performance of MiHomecare bore no resemblance to the past.

No reality check

The 2016 Mitie Annual Report shows that in that year sales at MiHomecare had actually fallen by 15% and that it had lurched into a significant loss of £8.6 million. This loss is shown in **Note 4 – Business and geographical segments** (above). Reality was significantly different from Mitie's future assumptions, it would seem. The goodwill balance for Mitie was pure fiction, reflecting vastly over-optimistic projections.

MITIE

Note 13: Goodwill, an extract

Goodwill has been allocated to CGUs, which align with the business segments, as this is how goodwill is monitored by the group internally. Goodwill has arisen principally on the acquisitions of Initial Security in 2006 (Soft FM). Dalkia Technical Facilities Management in 2009 (Hard FM) and Enara (Healthcare) in 2012.

	Discount rate 2016 %	Discount rate 2015 %	Goodwill 2016 £m	Goodwill 2015 £m
Soft FM	7.9	8.7	171.8	171.3
Hard FM	8.0	8.7	101.3	101.3
Property Management	9.2	10.0	85.2	85.2
Healthcare	9.1	10.0	107.2	106.6
			465.5	464.4

Source: 2016 Mitie Annual Report

Goodwill attached to Healthcare Divison – but it made losses in 2016

Note 13 – Goodwill (above and overleaf) from the 2016 Mitie Annual Report shows that 16% compound growth rates were expected from the healthcare division. This was unbelievable, especially as local authority funding for domiciliary care was falling and there was upward pressure on costs because of the minimum wage. Margins were going to be under pressure. Also unbelievable was Mitie's estimate that the recoverable amount for the healthcare division was £145 million (£107 million + £38 million), thereby justifying the carrying value of goodwill of £107 million. And yet only ten months after reporting that the

Note 13: Goodwill, an extract

> *Recoverable amount*
> *£107m + £38m = £145m*

The carrying value of goodwill relating to the Healthcare CGU of **£107.2m** (2015: £106.6m) was **£38.2m** less than the recoverable amount, being the net present value of the future cash flows that are expected to be generated by the business. These cash flow forecasts are derived from the detailed long-term business plan, with a terminal value using an inflationary growth rate assumption of 2.5% based on industry growth forecasts and compound annual revenue growth rates of **16%** (using revenue of £78.0m reported for the year ended 31 March 2016 as the reference point for the rate of compound annual revenue growth) underpinning the growth in operating profit in the first five years of the plan. The pre-tax rate used to discount the forecast cash flows for the CGU is 9.1%, which has been adjusted for the risks specific to the market in which the CGU operates.

Source: 2016 Mitie Annual Report

> *Plainly unbelievable in view of historic performance of the healthcare division, which made losses and had declining sales in 2016*

recoverable amount of the healthcare division was worth £145 million, Mitie announced that it had sold it for just £2. To add insult to the goodwill valuation injury, Mitie paid the buyers of MiHomecare a dowry of £9.5 million to get it off their hands.

Lesson

There was a great deal to worry about with the 2015 and 2016 Mitie Annual Reports. The very large subsequent prior year adjustments prove that point, but the unbelievably bullish assumptions made by management to justify the goodwill in the balance sheet for the healthcare division, MiHomecare, should have been enough in themselves to warn off potential shareholders. For management to have the pluck to forecast compound annual growth of 16% into the future for a healthcare division that had declined in sales by 15% in the previous year and was making significant losses, in order to justify its goodwill valuation of £107 million, seems to indicate a willingness to go to any accounting length to keep the Mitie show on the road. It has taken the arrival of excellent new management to put the numbers right. But oh what a wait it has been.

PART 5

Busy building less value

THE ACQUISITION ADDICTION

Marriages between companies start off with good intentions but rarely do they turn out the way management expected them to. Acquisitive companies often fail to deliver shareholder value and in general it is wise to avoid those that seem to be addicted to growth through acquisition. Big mergers that ended up destroying value include those of AOL and Time Warner, Vodafone and Mannesman, Compaq and Digital Equipment Corporation, Glaxo and SmithKlineBeecham. See also Slater and Gordon and Quindell (pages 87–93). In fact, according to a US study by Deloitte, if it is faster growth companies you are after, only a quarter or so of merger and acquisition deals actually deliver that.

Acquisitions fail to deliver for a host of reasons. There may be no logic to the deal. Why on earth did eBay buy Skype when the former's customers were happy to communicate by email? It may be management ego rather than business sense that is the driving force behind an acquisition, as with the Royal Bank of Scotland's

(RBS) record-breaking takeover of the Dutch banking group ABN AMRO in 2007, just before the global financial crisis. There must be logic to the deal and there must be thorough due diligence, especially of the accounts of the company being acquired – see Hewlett-Packard's acquisition of Autonomy (pages 55–62). The synergies need to be quantified and the integration thoroughly planned. The core business of the group must not be forgotten during the integration, and clients need to be managed through the process. There needs to be good and clear leadership and there must be communication within the newly enlarged group. Also, the right price must be paid – although there are plenty of examples of where it was not. The timing needs to be good in terms of the market cycles – which was certainly not the case for the RBS acquisition of ABN AMRO. The Bank of America acquisition of mortgage lender Countrywide in 2008 was also poorly timed, to say the least, as it was executed just before the global financial crisis and increased its exposure further to poor performing loans.

Another factor in all this is that the cultures of the two companies need to fit – which was not the case when the German car manufacturer BMW purchased the Rover Group from British Aerospace in 1994. Rover Group did not have a strong learning culture and had a 'not invented here' approach to the suggested improvements that were so desperately needed. Both Honda and BMW were after Rover. In the end, BMW won but did little due diligence and completed the acquisition in just ten days – although the BMW board was split on the merits of the deal.

It was the same for the motor manufacturers Daimler and Chrysler, whose merger never got into gear. The dudes in Detroit never got on with the sophisticates of Stuttgart and the merger failed largely because of the clash of cultures.

Tribal Group was a mishmash of a company that in one short period between 2002 and 2004 made nineteen acquisitions aimed at building up a conglomerate that could supply the public sector with any services it wanted. This was not a successful strategy, but the volume of acquisitions it made was clear to see from the annual reports and this in itself should have been a warning sign. Thankfully the company now has more focus and is flourishing.

In the 1990s Guardian IT was thought of as a fast-growing UK disaster recovery company, and as a result its shares were highly valued. But when it raised £134 million in 2000 to acquire a similar operation called Safetynet it became clear that its own business was not growing at all – in fact, it was going backwards – and it needed acquisitions to grow and maintain the high valuation of the shares. Quite rightly, companies that grow organically command higher valuations than those that grow by acquisition. The 2000 Guardian IT Annual Report showed that this highly rated company was not growing at all.

Conviviality was the same. Its core Bargain Booze chain of shops selling alcohol, tobacco and vaping products was not growing as fast as management wanted or had counted on. This prompted a move away from retailing to the wholesaling of drinks – an altogether different business with less attractive cash flow characteristics. It was a strategic mistake made worse by financial incompetence, which was plain to see when Conviviality took two stabs – the first in 2016, the second in 2017 – at calculating an onerous contract provision relating to three contracts.

As the former CEO of IBM, Louis V. Gerstner, once said: 'Successful enterprises are built from the ground up. You cannot assemble them with a bunch of acquisitions.'

Guardian IT

NO RECOVERY FROM DISASTER HERE

Over £1 billion! That's what Guardian IT was worth in 2000 at the height of the tech bubble. Two years later, after accounting irregularities were uncovered by a new finance director, followed by the inevitable subsequent share price collapse, SunGard Data Systems of the US put both Guardian IT and its many well-known institutional investors out of their misery by buying the company for 5% of what it had been worth at its peak.

Guardian IT specialised in disaster recovery services – providing its clients with computer systems and work stations in the event of their own systems going down as a result of, say, a fire or a terrorist act. The trouble was that, while Guardian IT was busy preparing for its clients' disasters, it was also creating a disaster of its own, thanks to a very aggressive acquisition policy and poor accounting. The company's shares may have been riding high, but there was no growth in profits from its core activities. The growth reported was the result of very expensive acquisitions and it could only continue for as long as investors were happy to stump up more cash. Whilst there were no telltale signs in the 2000 Guardian IT Annual Report of the accounting problems to

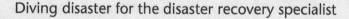
Diving disaster for the disaster recovery specialist

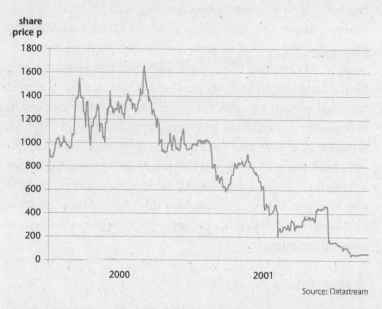

Source: Datastream

come, the absence of cash generation and a lack of organic growth showed that the company was clearly reliant on acquisitions to grow. That should in itself have been enough of a warning sign, especially for a company whose share price was already potentially overvalued.

Acquisitions were no safety net

Guardian IT made acquisitions in 2000. In June it undertook the biggest rights issue of that year to date on the London market, raising £134 million to assist in the purchase of Safetynet, another company involved in disaster recovery, for £170 million. The acquisition certainly kept earnings moving ahead in the year that it was acquired, but it was purchased at a not very safety-first price of over seventy times earnings – and it had no assets. Indeed, a basic Companies House search would have revealed that profits at Safetynet had not grown at all in the previous two years. So why did Guardian IT pay so much for it? It did not take long for the management at Guardian IT to realise that it had overpaid and, eighteen months after the acquisition, the value ascribed to Safetynet in Guardian IT's accounts was reduced by £63 million, resulting in a huge loss for 2001. The optimistic estimates for 2001 sales and profits made at the time of the acquisition had not materialised, and so a write-down of the large amount of goodwill was required. This was strange as, at the time of its acquisition by Guardian IT, Safetynet apparently had significant forward contract income.

A new finance director

As is sometimes the case, the hasty departure of a finance director and the swift arrival of a new one raises unanticipated issues. That was certainly the case for Guardian IT. Carillion (see page 162), Amey (see page 146) and iSoft (see page 69) are other good examples of companies where new finance directors raised issues that observers had been highlighting for some time. Within seventeen days of his arrival, the new finance director at Guardian IT, Neil Roberts, had reduced expectations for 2001 because forecast sales were overly optimistic and costs had been under-estimated. By the time he had been in the job for seventy-four days Roberts had identified discrepancies that required adjust-ments to the accounts and the addition of further exceptional costs. The most significant adjustment was the write-down in value of Guardian IT's web-hosting activities, which had only just been established at Heathrow Airport. Seemingly £15 million had been spent on this in 2001, but it all had to be written off in the same year. Roberts also warned that the company's goodwill valuation needed to be reduced and its banking covenants relaxed. The chairman resigned. Guardian IT subsequently reported a loss of £95 million for 2001, while the previously reported profit of £4 million for 2000 was restated as a loss of £3 million. Roberts certainly had an effect.

Fortunately for shareholders, in 2002 a leading US disaster recovery specialist, SunGard Data Systems, bid 80p for Guardian IT and the banks got their money back. Let's be clear: none of what the new finance director discovered on his arrival was obvious from the 2000 Guardian IT Annual Report, but investors should have been wary well ahead of his appointment because the annual report showed that there had been no organic growth in profits. Cash flow was also very poor, as could be seen from the rising interest costs the company was paying in spite of continually raising finance through the issue of shares.

No growth, but investors still bought the shares

In 2000 there were virtually no blue chip investors on the Guardian IT share register. But by the end of 2001, when the shares had completed much of their dive, it had a whole raft of new, well-known institutional shareholders. Just as a rising tide lifts all boats, the contrary is true too: a falling tide (or share price) can leave boats (or investors, in Guardian IT's case) high and dry, especially if the shares become illiquid and difficult to trade in. And so it was for some big money fund managers. But

Consolidated profit and loss account
for the year ended 31 December 2000, £'000

	Continuing 2000	Acquisitions 2000	Total 2000	Total 1999
Turnover	67,501	18,896	86,397	49,245
Cost of sales	(21,971)	(6,495)	(28,466)	(16,656)
Gross profit	45,530	12,401	57,931	32,589
Administrative expenses	(36,858)	(13,426)	(50,284)	(23,499)
Operating profit before goodwill amortisation and exceptional costs	11,227	5,782	17,009	10,368
Goodwill amortisation	(2,555)	(5,891)	(8446)	(1,278)
Exceptional costs	–	(916)	(916)	–
Operating profit/(loss)	8,672	(1,025)	7,647	9,090
Share of operating profit in associate			105	20
Total operating profit:				
Group and share of associate			7,752	9,110
Net interest			(3,895)	(2,062)
Profit on ordinary activities before taxation, goodwill amortisation and exceptional costs			13,219	8,326

Source: 2000 Guardian IT Annual Report

Operating profit before goodwill and exceptional costs	17,009	10,368
Less acquisitions	(5,782)	–
	11,227	10,368
Less interest	(3,895)	(2,062)
	7,332	8,306

An 11% decline in profits from core activities

what attracted them to Guardian IT in the first place? A simple analysis of the 2000 Guardian IT Annual Report tells us that its growth came from acquisitions. The consolidated profit and loss account in the 2000 Guardian IT Annual Report (opposite) shows this.

Simply by adjusting 2000 operating profits by the contribution reported from acquisitions, Guardian IT's core activities went backwards by 11%. But new investors must have bought the shares at a historical price earnings ratio of between thirty and seventy times – pricey for a company showing negative growth in its core activities that was none the less very keen to splash shares around in order to raise cash for acquisitions. This should have been enough to deter experienced investors, who should have known that if growth is chiefly coming from acquisitions this can be manipulated in the short term, and it is often only a matter of time before the music stops and the weakness in the core activities is exposed. This was a significant warning sign, in particular since the shares were so highly valued. Typically, companies that are highly acquisitive are often rated lower in valuation terms than companies that are growing organically. Guardian IT appeared to break this rule.

Lesson

Companies that rely on acquisitions for growth need to be treated with caution. Profits can be manipulated in the short term through the use of fair value adjustments in the acquired company, the timing of revenues and costs, and the use of provisions. Highly valued companies whose growth is reliant on acquisitions should be avoided in particular. Guardian IT was a good example of this.

Tribal Group

TOO MANY TRIBES

What a mishmash of a company Tribal Group was. It claimed at various times to be involved in human resources, services to central government and local government, consultancy, health and social care, social housing, communications and PR, property services, IT, training, oh and don't forget education services. Far too many tribes, when many would argue that to be successful you must have focus.

In 2004 and again in 2015, shareholders in the group suffered dramatic falls in the value of their shares. I recall coming away from a meeting with the directors of Tribal Group in 2003 with the firm belief that there was no way the company could keep all its acquisition plates spinning. It didn't, which is hardly surprising given that in the two years to March 2004 Tribal Group made nineteen acquisitions that did not seem to fit together and it spent up to £150 million doing so. Paying for such acquisitions in both cash and shares meant that a flow of paper was always going to keep the lid on share price appreciation.

Following the acquisition fest of the past and the loss to shareholder value that resulted, Tribal Group changed its strategy to

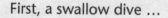

First, a swallow dive ...

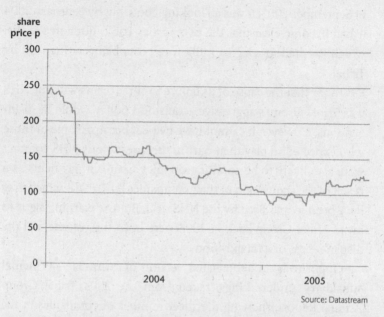

Source: Datastream

focus on providing education services and software. The transition could not be termed 'best in class' and in 2015 Tribal yet again disappointed the market when profit expectations were not met because a number of large contracts proved more difficult to execute than had been anticipated. But it is good news that there is now only one tribe at Tribal Group, which provides services and software to educational establishments throughout the world. This tribe has focus and therefore has a chance of survival in the business jungle.

Through acquisitions, Tribal Group built up a healthcare division it called Mercury Health. This division entered into discussions with the NHS to set up a chain of national treatment centres and was appointed the preferred bidder for the contract in September 2003. It was all looking good, but by February 2004 it had become clear that the two parties could not agree terms, which resulted in over £5 million of costs being written off by Tribal.

To say that the cause of its failure to agree terms with the NHS was Tribal Group's aggressive acquisition policy would be disingenuous. However, it cannot have helped, because some of those who expected to play their part in this prestigious NHS contract were also likely to be counting on juicy earn-out payments as a result of the acquisition of their companies by Tribal – which may have been jeopardised by the NHS deal. But the warning signs to avoid Tribal Group back in 2004 were both the volume and the disparateness of its acquisitions.

Opposite is an abbreviated version of **Note 31 – Principal subsidiary undertakings**, taken from the 2004 Tribal Group Annual Report, showing the sheer number of companies in the group. This actually understates Tribal Group's acquisition frenzy at the time, as it does not include companies which were acquired and subsequently closed and their staff assimilated into existing activities. It was therefore only a matter of time before Tribal Group unravelled, as a highly acquisitive strategy that does not integrate companies effectively and knit the new group together nearly always destroys shareholder value. It is worth perusing the principal activities of Tribal Group's subsidiary undertakings and consider how on earth these were supposed to fit together. What could possibly be the synergies and business logic in putting a recruiter, an architect, a software company, an Ofsted inspection company and a library management company in the same group?

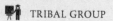

Note 31: Principal subsidiary undertakings, an extract

Subsidiary	Principal activity	Holding
Action Medical Ltd	Recruitment to the medical profession	100%
Atlas Media Group Ltd	PR consultants	100%
Ben Johnson-Hill Associates Ltd	Benchmarking services	100%
Cambridge Training	Multi-media training	100%
Tribal Dundas Consultancy Services Ltd	Further education consultancy	100%
FD Learning Ltd	Software and support services	77%
Foundation Software Solutions Ltd	Supplier of software	77%
Geronimo Public Relations Ltd	Public relations consultancy	100%
HACAS Group Ltd	Housing regeneration consultancy	100%
Instant Library Ltd	Library and information management	100%
Kingsway Advertising Ltd	Design and advertising agency	100%
Network Training Publishing Ltd	Producer of training course materials	100%
Network Training (Taunton) Ltd	Further education and consultancy	100%
Nightingale Architects Ltd	Architects	100%
Secta Group Ltd	Management consultancy	100%
SfE Ltd	Teacher training and distance learning	100%
Tribal Asset Management Ltd	Asset management software	100%
Tribal Consulting Ltd	Management consultancy	100%
Tribal Education Ltd	Education consultancy	100%
Tribal GWT Group Ltd	Recruitment and search and selection	85%
Tribal Holdings Ltd	Holding company	100%
Tribal PPI Group Ltd	Ofsted inspections	100%
Tribal Property Services Ltd	Property consultants	100%
Tribal Technology Ltd	Software support and IT services	77%
Yale Data Management Consultants Ltd	Management and IT consultants	100%

Source: 2004 Tribal Group Annual Report

One of the most useful routines in analysing a company's accounts is to run one's fingers slowly down the two columns of numbers that make up the income statement and balance sheet which give the figures for the most recent year alongside those of the previous year. Any major change from one year to the next needs to be fully understood in the context of the activity level in

... and then a high cliff dive

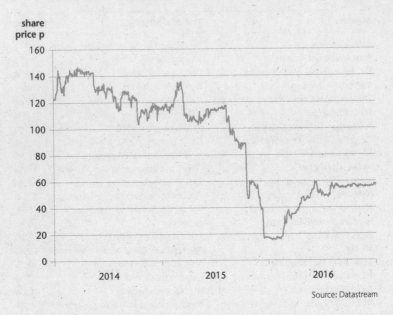

Source: Datastream

sales of the company in that year. The notes to the accounts give more colour to these numbers – as was certainly the case in the 2014 Tribal Group Annual Report.

Note 20 – Trade and other receivables (opposite) in the 2014 Tribal Group Annual Report tells us that, whilst trade and other receivables in 2012, 2013 and 2014 changed little, their make-up certainly did. The quality of these assets seriously deteriorated in 2014, which was a warning sign of bad things to come.

As we have seen with many of the other companies in this book, a big rise in accrued income is nearly always a worry. It's a management estimate of what they think is owed to the company for work done. It is not supported by invoices and it is difficult to

Note 20: Trade and other receivables, an extract, £'000

	2014	2013	2012
Amounts receivable for the sale of goods and services	13,217	18,492	16,823
Allowance for doubtful debts	(153)	(216)	(287)
	13,064	18,276	16,536
Amounts recoverable on contracts	115	270	812
Other receivables	294	283	903
Prepayments	3,822	2,705	2,353
Accrued income	10,842	7,381	7,621
	28,137	28,915	28,225

Source: 2014 Tribal Group Annual Report

Large fall in invoiced receivables

Significant rise in uninvoiced receivables – accrued income

audit. However, it is also often pure profit, especially in a software business where the costs have already passed through the income statement. No surprise then that, four months after filing the 2014 Tribal Group Annual Report, management said that they had 'seen the extension of certain large customer programme timelines, which has resulted in the deferral of revenue and higher project delivery costs'. For which, read the clients were not happy, they were not paying, and the company needed to do more to deliver on projects.

There were plenty of other worrying signs in the 2014 Tribal Group Annual Report, including nearly £20 million of costs in Note 6 under 'Other Items' – a tally of previous expensive mistakes by management.

Lesson

Tribal Group is alive and well now and has a focus – something that its previous managements failed to achieve. It was bailed out by a 1 for 1 rights issue at 22p in March 2016 that refinanced the company. Without this injection of funds, it may well have gone bust. But the lesson is clear: avoid highly acquisitive companies and those that accrue (for which, read estimate!) large amounts of sales. The latter is a familiar warning sign that often pre-empts a dramatic fall in a share price.

Conviviality

TWO BITES AT THE CHERRY(ADE)

They must have been under the influence. Why anyone was tempted to invest in Conviviality after its dramatic change of focus was a mystery. Those that did and who – unlike the sober investors at Artemis and Schroders – failed to see what was going wrong are now nursing an investment hangover. Conviviality bombed out and went dramatically bust in 2018. But there were warning signs. Its core retail businesses, which comprised Bargain Booze, Wine Rack and Select Convenience, were going nowhere. Already a low-margin business, its sales were actually going backwards in some periods. And then it changed its strategy.

The story starts in 2013, when new management were brought in to Conviviality by its private equity owners to revamp its Bargain Booze retail franchise chain, develop a sober strategy for growth, and to float the company on AIM. Bargain Booze sold beers, wines, spirits, soft drinks, convenience food, tobacco and popular vaping products. Its heartland was the north-west of England and the plan was to roll out Bargain Booze outlets across the UK. The management's view was that many people in the UK these days could not be bothered to drive to the supermarket for their booze, preferring to pop round the corner to a convenience store. Bargain Booze aimed to capitalise on this perceived change in shopping habits by opening new sites, but in order to do this it needed access to finance.

Following the listing of the shares on AIM, Bargain Booze changed its name to Conviviality and a series of acquisitions followed. The acquisition strategy included taking on debt and raising money through the issue of new shares at a staggering rate. At its peak, Conviviality was a well-oiled share-issuing machine and, to be fair, this was enough to frighten off many of the established smaller company investors who had been big fans of the new and confident management team. Surprisingly, though, some hung on to their shares to the bitter end.

At its flotation in July 2013, Conviviality, which at the time consisted of no more than the chain of Bargain Booze outlets, was worth just £70 million. In the three subsequent years, Conviviality acquired the retailers Wine Rack (£2 million), GT News (£6 million), Rhythm and Booze (£2 million); the drinks wholesaler Matthew Clark (£200 million); and the wine merchant Bibendum (£60 million). Late in 2017, Conviviality acquired yet another retailer, Central Convenience (£30 million), although this did not disguise the fact that the company's business strategy had changed from retailing to one with an increased emphasis on wholesaling.

At its peak in late 2017, Conviviality was worth nearly £750 million as some bought into the original strategy and then were convinced by an entirely different one. By April 2018, Conviviality was worth nothing.

Management's original strategy was to build a large chain of franchisee-operated retail convenience outlets focused on the Bargain Booze and Wine Rack brands. Customers paid cash and

Share price falls under the influence

share
price p

Source: Datastream

Conviviality took credit from its suppliers. As long as the margins and sales held up, this was a model that could produce positive profits and cash flow.

But the expected growth did not materialise and so, to plaster over the cracks in its business strategy, Conviviality purchased two large wholesalers. They believed that by combining retailing with wholesaling there were significant synergies to be had in terms of organisational efficiencies, better buying and economies in distribution costs, and that additional revenue could be generated.

This change in strategy proved to be a big mistake. This was because drink wholesaling, like drink retailing, is a low-margin business but with added cash flow disadvantages, as firms like

Matthew Clark and Bibendum supply hotels, restaurants and pubs on credit.

Time, gentlemen, please

March 2018 heralded a string of announcements that ultimately resulted in 'Time, gentlemen, please' being called for Conviviality.

First there was the admission that there had been a £5 million arithmetical error in compiling the profit forecasts for 2018. Those who had subscribed for shares at 375p only a few months earlier for the £30 million acquisition of Central Convenience were particularly aggrieved. There was also an admission that wholesale margins had fallen.

A week after this announcement, Conviviality confessed to forgetting to accrue for £30 million of tax on tobacco and alcohol. How can you forget this? Surely it is accrued for and paid to HMRC like clockwork on a regular basis. Furthermore, there was also a funding requirement, as the company had run out of banking facilities. Its shares were suspended. Conviviality was teetering like a drunk.

Diana Hunter, Conviviality's assertive chief executive, left and the non-executive chairman, David Adams, stepped up to the task of raising £125 million to pay what was owed to suppliers and HMRC, as well as to repay the £30 million revolving credit facilities in full and ensure that there was enough working capital.

There were further downgrades of expectations, with little growth expected from the business as a whole – which is hardly surprising, given that none of the businesses it had acquired had previously shown signs of any real growth.

By the end of March 2018, Conviviality announced that it had failed to raise the £125 million from shareholders that was needed to refinance the company. Last orders were called and administrators were appointed. The UK's largest franchised off-licence chain, which was also the UK's largest independent drinks wholesaler, had gone bust. The end was fast. Conviviality took little more than a month to keel over.

Two bites at the cherry(ade)

There were plenty of signs that Conviviality was not as welcoming a company to investors as its name implied. It was highly acquisitive and kept on issuing shares, implying banks were wary; Note 14 – Trade and other receivables in the 2017 Conviviality Annual Report showed that it had £42 million of trade receivables that were overdue but not impaired, raising questions about revenue recognition; it changed its strategy significantly when its original one failed to deliver; it was not cash generative and this deteriorated further following the acquisitions of the two large wholesaling businesses; in most years there was an emphasis on adjusted profits and earnings that excluded large exceptional costs; the original private equity owners sold all their shares at IPO; and management owned virtually no shares. These were all reasons enough to be cautious, though of course none of them could tell us that the company was going to fail to provide for tax due to HMRC. The natural assumption would have been that the accounts included an accrual for the large amounts of duty paid by customers on alcohol and tobacco, which was then payable by Conviviality to HMRC.

But the real reason for caution was the liberal use of provisions – clear from the 2017 Conviviality Annual Report – on the

Note 28: Business combinations
Matthew Clark (Holdings) Limited, an extract, £'000

The following table summarises the consideration paid for Matthew Clark (Holdings) Limited, and the amount of assets acquired and liabilities assumed recognised at the acquisition date.

	Book value	Fair value adjustment	Fair value
Property, plant and equipment	4,074	(891)	3,183
Intangible assets	3,624	(311)	3,313
Inventories	44,238	(266)	43,972
Trade and other receivables	116,738	(359)	116,379
Net debt and debt-like items	(10,838)	(247)	(11,085)
Trade and other payables	(122,979)	(1,084)	(124,063)
Derivatives	(634)	–	(634)
Deferred tax liability	402	(11,859)	(11,457)
Provisions	(603)	(5,167)	(5,770)
Total identifiable net assets	34,022	(20,184)	13,838
Allocation to intangible assets – brands			23,900
Allocation to intangible assets – customer base			38,800
Goodwill			122,438
Total consideration satisfied by cash			198,976

Source: 2016 Conviviality Annual Report

> *Original provisions made for onerous contracts at Matthew Clark*

acquisition of Matthew Clark. This told us a lot about the way the company was being managed. Because of widespread abuse in the past by highly acquisitive companies, provisions cannot be made for future losses or for reorganisation costs to be incurred following an acquisition of one company by another. Once upon a time this ruse was used to keep costs away from the important earnings figure to ensure a company kept reporting a progressive positive trend. Under IFRS 3 – Business Combinations, introduced in January 2008, an acquirer can now only recognise an acquiree's liabilities at fair value if they existed at the acquisition date.

IFRS 3 – Business Combinations says that the assets and liabilities of an acquired company must be recognised in the acquirer's accounts at fair value. This allows liabilities such as onerous contracts to be recognised as they existed at the time of acquisition. And so it was for Conviviality's strategy-changing acquisition of Matthew Clark in 2015. The accounts provide £5.2 million for the onerous contracts inherited at Matthew Clark in the results for 2016 – all above board and shown in **Note 28 – Business combinations** (opposite).

The trouble was that Conviviality had two bites at the cherry(ade). In the results for 2017, and shown in **Note 28 – Business combinations, continued** (see next page) they had another stab at calculating the provision for these onerous contracts, this time putting it at £11.0 million. They had already had ten months to work out the fair value of the provision for the three contracts the first time they had calculated it. That is long enough. To have to go back to the contracts twenty-two months later and say that they had got it wrong and it needed increasing tells you all you need to know about the quality of the management, in particular the finance team. Perhaps not so surprising, then, that they forgot to accrue for £30 million of tax and perhaps also not so surprising that they got their arithmetic wrong by £5 million in forecasting for the 2018 profit estimates. The warning signs were there in 2017.

Conviviality is another example of the Iceberg Principle in

Note 28: Business combinations, continued
Prior business combinations
Matthew Clark (Holdings) Limited, an extract, £'000

The following table summarises the consideration paid for Matthew Clark (Holdings) Limited, and the amount of assets acquired and liabilities assumed recognised at the acquisition date.

	Book value	Fair value adjustment	Fair value
Property, plant and equipment	4,074	(891)	3,183
Intangible assets	3,624	(311)	3,313
Inventories	44,238	(266)	43,972
Trade and other receivables	116,738	(359)	116,379
Net debt and debt-like items	(10,838)	(247)	(11,085)
Trade and other payables	(122,979)	(1,084)	(124,063)
Derivatives	(634)	–	(634)
Deferred tax liability	402	(10,080)	(9,678)
Provisions	(603)	**(10,991)**	(11,594)
Total identifiable net assets	34,022	(24,229)	9,793
Allocation to intangible assets – brands			23,900
Allocation to intangible assets – customer base			38,800
Goodwill			126,483
Total consideration satisfied by cash			198,976

Source: 2017 Conviviality Annual Report

Two bites of the cherry – increased provisions made for onerous contracts at Matthew Clark operation. If you can see one problem in an annual report, there are likely to be others lurking out of sight below the water line. If you had sold Conviviality shares when this extra provision was reported, you would have got about 360p per share. Less than nine months later, the shares were worthless.

The Financial Reporting Council (FRC) is currently investigating the audit of the financial statements of Conviviality for the year ended April 2017 and the preparation and approval of the financial statements. The auditors KPMG believe that they conducted the audit appropriately and are cooperating fully with the enquiry.

Lesson

There were plenty of signs that Conviviality was not the friendly and congenial investment its name implies. Those who were persuaded to invest in it by its self-assured management and who failed to spot the warning signs when its strategy changed, suffered large losses. Of course, no forensic analysis of the company's annual report would have told you that management would fail in its most basic of duties to accrue for a regular payment of tax. But revisiting fair value provisions in 2017 for three onerous contracts, having first been made aware of them twenty-two months previously, should have told you more than enough about the accounting practices at Conviviality, quite apart from the very odd £42 million of trade receivables that were overdue but not impaired. If they could get the provisions so wrong, they could get more serious stuff wrong. Which they did.

PART 6

Never mind the width, feel the quality

DETERIORATING ASSETS

There were big similarities between Amey and Carillion. There was overlap, too, with the UK's current biggest outsourcing company, Capita. But it was surprising that Carillion was ever allowed to get into the state that it did and go bust. Surely governments, customers, auditors, regulators, bankers and investors learn from history? Both the UK's main political parties have in their time enthusiastically embraced public finance initiative (PFI) contracts, as they have allowed them to get hospitals, schools, bridges and such like built without the government having to dip into its capital budgets. PFI has been good for the government balance sheet, but highly contentious for lots of other reasons.

Let's be clear. There are very few similarities between what were once the UK's largest outsourcing companies and Aston Martin Lagonda (AML). But there was one. Amey, Carillion and Capita all demonstrated a decline over time in the quality of their current assets. This is important as current assets should turn into cash. AML, at the time of its flotation on the London Stock Exchange, increased its credit period to its dealers from 34 days to 47 days – a 38% increase. It has risen dramatically since then. The luxury motor vehicles at the dealers rose significantly indicating that future sales might be difficult to obtain as the channel looked to be full. We now know this is exactly what happened, as although retail sales at AML distributors have advanced, sales to them have definitely not. There may also be revenue recognition issues because the luxury motor vehicles may need to be returned to make way for newer models like the much heralded DBX SUV – AML's four wheel drive car.

It was Amey that went virtually bust in 2003, during the period of the Labour government's most enthusiastic support for PFI, but luckily for everyone involved the Spanish multinational Ferrovial stepped in and bid for the company after the share price had fallen 90% in nine months. At least shareholders were able to claw something back and subcontractors were paid. Carillion was an Amey doppelgänger in so many ways, the difference being that, when it went into liquidation in January 2018, there was no bidder to pick up the pieces and it was a Conservative government in power this time round. Carillion's subcontractors, bankers and shareholders, perhaps believing that the government would not let one of its chief contractors go to the wall, got nothing. As many people have pointed out, Capita is no Carillion, but there are similarities in the way the current assets recorded in the annual reports of both companies deteriorated over time. There are similarities in the client base, too, with both having significant exposure to the public sector and substantial projects in the UK and abroad.

Whilst there was more construction at Carillion than there was at Amey, and it was this activity that it found so problematic, the main markets that both these companies rendered services to were virtually identical in the UK. Let's list the similarities: both companies had significant activities in transport, PFI contracts, roads, rail, utilities, defence, education, health and facilities management. Vast tranches of both companies' revenues, and therefore their profits, were dependent on the application of IAS 18 – Revenue, in that they 'rendered services' to their clients, which often straddled a number of accounting periods, and IAS 11 – Construction Contracts, as they undertook construction contracts which also straddled a number of accounting periods.

When the outcome of a contract for rendering services can be estimated reliably, the amount of revenue recognised should be by reference to the stage of completion of the contract at the end of the year – this is often called the 'percentage of completion' method. The outcome of the rendering of services can be estimated reliably if all the following are satisfied:

- Revenue can be measured reliably.
- It is probable that the economic benefits related to the contract will flow to the seller.
- The costs so far incurred and the costs required in order to complete the contract can be measured reliably.
- The stage of completion of the contract can be measured reliably at the end of the accounting period.

The stage of completion therefore needs to be determined. This can be done through surveys or by examining the extent of services performed to date as a percentage of the total services to be performed, or by working out the proportion of the costs incurred to date as a proportion of the total costs of the contract.

IAS 11 says that revenues and costs – which together determine the profit – should be recognised as the contract progresses. Determining the progress of the contract can require a great deal of judgement. As one can see from the requirements of IAS 18 and IAS 11, a considerable reliance is put on measuring and on estimates and judgements that can often be wrong. This partly explains why both Amey and Carillion lurched into very significant losses once a fresh pair of eyes was introduced. For Amey the fresh pair of eyes came in the form of Eric Tracey, a temporary finance director seconded from Deloitte & Touche, who was parachuted into the company to get to grips with its support service and construction contracts. On his watch the legacy of the past mismanagement was corrected and a new conservative accounting regime was installed, under which Amey reported losses of £129 million in 2002. In 2003, £223 million of receivable balances, included in current assets in the balance sheet and previously thought of as good, were written down.

Following the departure from Carillion of two finance directors, Richard Adam and Zafar Khan, and its chief executive, Richard Howson, a non-executive director, Keith Cochrane, became interim chief executive, while Emma Mercer – seen by many as a whistleblower – took over as finance director. They made a massive £1 billion provision against many of the construction and support service receivables included as current assets in Carillion's balance sheet which had only months earlier been given a clean bill of health by the auditors.

Eric Tracey at Amey and Keith Cochrane and Emma Mercer at Carillion reviewed their respective inherited balance sheets based on previous managements' measurements, estimates and judgements and concluded very swiftly that many of these were plain wrong. But to many observers this had been obvious for a time and, while the new bosses at the troubled companies had the benefit of looking at many of the contracts in detail and formulating their own views as to their value, the fast-deteriorating asset quality seen in the current assets of their respective annual reports in the years immediately before the companies started to collapse were warning signs that both Amey and Carillion shares were to be avoided.

The lessons of the collapse of Amey, Carillion – and indeed others in the construction and support services sector – are that IAS 18 – Revenue, and IAS 11 – Construction Contracts, are totally inadequate and need replacing, as they rely too much on management estimates and judgements and on measurements which are too easily manipulated to achieve targets rather than reflecting the reality of the situation. IFRS 15 – Revenue from Contracts with Customers, a new and much-needed accounting standard which became effective in January 2018, will help do this. This new accounting standard sets some criteria where one can recognise revenue over time, but in most cases revenue is recognised at a point in time when agreed performance obligations have been achieved. In simple terms this means that in future revenues will be recognised more in line with when cash is received from the client. The mismatch of profits and cash flow, so often seen when companies are overstating the former, is less likely to arise post the adoption of IFRS 15. One wonders why this did not come into force sooner, but it is none the less welcome.

Amey

INTERLOCKING WEAKNESSES

'Interlocking Strengths' – that was the company mantra proudly stamped across the front cover of the 2001 Amey Annual Report, published just before its shares started their precipitous fall. 'Interlocking weaknesses', more like.

Amey provided support services to a wide range of government organisations and private sector companies. It operated in a broad range of sectors, including rail, highways, defence, health, local government, utilities and education, many of which were serviced through PFIs – at the time a popular way for government to arrange financing for big capital projects. PFIs allow the government access to private sector finance in order to enable infrastructure such as hospitals to be built. The government does not have to fork out for the capital costs of building a hospital but in return its (and future governments') hands are tied into paying for its use once the hospital becomes available for use. In the short term, the capital expenditure is kept off the government's balance sheet. In the longer term, government has to find more out of its budget for current expenditure in order to pay for using the hospital.

Amey's strategic aim was by all accounts to become a FTSE 100

Share price reaction to large asset write downs

share
price p

Source: Datastream

company, but some said that it lacked the strategic thinking on the nuts and bolts of how to get there. Part of the problem was that, like Carillion (see page 162), Amey was not selective enough about the work it bid for, taking on big contracts that had large upfront costs and which often took longer than expected to complete – which inevitably put pressure on its already stretched balance sheet. The company concentrated on contracts that looked as if they would make decent margins, but it had scant regard for the timings of cash flows – much like other UK support service companies, it would appear.

When asked in 2002 about Amey's continuing accounting changes, the finance director at the time, David Miller, said that the prospect of having to deal with a whole new draft of thirty-two accounting standards was as appealing as 'a little cup of sick and I'm not going to drink it'. Amey unravelled after he resigned in September 2002, as the new finance director wrote down assets that had previously been recognised as income.

Miller was replaced as finance director by Michael Kayser, who, having looked at the numbers, left after just five weeks. In desperation, management turned to Eric Tracey, an experienced audit partner from Deloitte & Touche, (now Deloitte LLP), to act as finance director and prepare the results for 2002. Tracey was subsequently named UK New Zealander of the Year and for his work at Amey he was shortlisted in 2003 as Finance Director of the Year by *Accountancy Age*. He went on to become finance director of Wembley, a British gaming company with interests in American casinos, at a time when it faced legal actions in the US. More recently he has been appointed as a non-executive director at problematical Findel (see page 217). Clearly Tracey likes a challenge.

Tracey certainly put his extensive accountancy training into practice, as Amey reported losses in 2002 of £129 million, mostly made up of current asset write-downs where previously the company had been too optimistic as to their recovery. A perusal of the 2001 Amey Annual Report, in particular **Note 19 – Debtors** (see page 152) would have shown that it was only a matter of time before this overstatement of debtors needed to be adjusted. Tracey did just that.

The arrival of Tracey only hastened Amey's demise. An extract from the 2002 Amey Annual Report, shown opposite, details the exceptional items prepared by Tracey. It adjusts for many of the obvious overstatements of assets seen in the 2001 Amey Annual Report. Tracey was just setting the accounts straight.

Financial review: Exceptional items, an extract, £m

The results for the year are also dominated by the following exceptional charges made in arriving at operating profit but which are excluded from the tables above and are summarised below:

	Continuing core	Continuing being discontinued	Discontinued	Total
Current asset write downs	(4.9)	**(69.9)**	–	(74.8)
Dispute settlements	(6.7)	–	–	(6.7)
Investment write downs		**(19.5)**	–	(19.5)
Advisers' fees relating to covenant renegotiation	(8.0)	–	–	(8.0)
Strategic review and restructuring costs	(3.7)	–	(0.9)	(4.6)
	(23.3)	(89.4)	(0.9)	(113.6)
Loss on sale of subsidiaries	–	–	(7.9)	(7.9)
Total (pre-tax)	**(23.3)**	**(89.4)**	**(8.8)**	**(121.5)**
Taxation	2.4	8.8	0.1	11.3
Total (post tax)	**(20.9)**	**(80.6)**	**(8.7)**	**(110.2)**

Source: 2002 Amey Annual Report

> Write down in value of construction projects

> Write down in value of joint ventures – mainly Croydon Trams

The Iceberg Principle in reverse

In the world of forensic accounting, the Iceberg Principle is the term used when, on close examination of a company's annual report, you spot one accounting horror but you also have the whiff of other shenanigans. As with an iceberg, you can see only the tip of the problem as the bulk remains hidden below the water line – but one accounting horror should be enough to warn you to steer away. With Amey, however, it was a case of the Iceberg Principle in reverse because most of the accounting issues were in plain sight and there for all to see.

Let me list a few of the issues in the 2001 Amey Annual Report:

- Amey restated results for 2000 in order to account for revenue from joint ventures more conservatively; this reduced previously reported profits by £14.9 million.

- It changed its accounting policy on pre-contract costs, so that they were no longer capitalised but expensed through the income statement as they were incurred; this reduced previously reported profits by £7–8 million.

- Amey also restated previous results for 1999 in order to account for bid costs to be recognised in the year in which they were incurred.

- Over time, Amey turned pension fund assets into liabilities – sounds familiar.

- Amey was highly leveraged and had very poor cash flow, although this was partially masked by increasing use of debt and the issue of shares.

- There were large amounts of receivables from customers that were due in more than a year's time – often a sign of trouble ahead.

- Amey had odd arrangements with some joint ventures – see the J J Gallagher deal covered later in this chapter.

- It was the joint ventures, which were impossible to analyse from the annual report, that reported profits, not Amey's core activities.

- Amey paid shareholders dividends that were not supported by earnings – an unsustainable situation.

In other words, there were warning signs everywhere. Just one of these issues alone should have been enough to scare off even the most risk-seeking investor. It was surprising that so many government bodies dealt with Amey, but the herd instinct comes to mind. As they used to say in the early days of office computers, 'No one ever got fired for buying from IBM.' The only problem here was that Amey was no IBM.

The restatement of results turned a profit before tax for 2000 of £27 million into just £6 million, and transformed a profit before tax for 1999 of £7 million into a £2 million loss. With this restatement of previous years' reported results, investors were now perhaps entitled to believe that Amey had brought its accounting practices into line. But no – the 2001 Amey Annual Report raised a number of issues that should have continued to worry them.

Deteriorating asset quality

In 2001 the company reported a loss of £18 million, but **Note 19 – Debtors** (see next page) in the annual report for that year shows the most significant issue – deteriorating asset quality. Long-term receivables and accrued income amounts doubled from 2000 to 2001 – a clear sign that there may be trouble ahead. Amey had taken credit for the revenue associated with these assets in its income statement but was not expecting to receive much of the cash until a year later.

Note 19: Debtors, £'000

	Group 2001	Restated group 2000
Amounts falling due within one year		
Trade debtors	102,048	50,645
Amounts recoverable on contracts	97,946	154,827
Amounts owed by subsidiary undertakings	–	–
Corporation tax	2, 890	–
Other debtors	**19,245**	**15,787**
Prepayments and accrued income	**17,079**	**12,528**
	239,208	233,787
Amounts falling due after more than one year		
Amounts receivable on contracts	**21,600**	**–**
Accrued income	**12,550**	**4,804**
Deferred tax asset:		
– unutilised tax losses carried forward	9,997	9,460
– accelerated capital allowances	1,029	–
– other reversing timing differences	1,383	–
	46,559	14,246

Source: 2001 Amey Annual Report

£70,474	£33,119

A doubling of lower quality assets from 2000 to 2001

Note 17: Investments in joint ventures, £'000

	2001	2000
Amounts outstanding from joint ventures		
Loans to joint ventures:		
3ED Glasgow Limited	6,644	923
Tramtrack Croydon Limited	3,858	1,016
	10,502	1,939

During the year, the Group entered into an agreement with J J Gallagher Ltd, under which it agreed a **£20 million** fee for the procurement of services to be provided by the Group in future years. The Group has subsequently agreed that payment for these services will be deferred over a five year period.

In related agreements signed since the year end, the Group has made an initial investment of **£8 million** for 19% of a company related to J J Gallagher Ltd and entered into a commitment to invest up to an additional **£12 million** over five years dependent upon performance. The Group may make additional investments dependent upon further agreement with J J Gallagher Ltd.

Source: 2001 Amey Annual Report

> £8 million +
> £12 million =
> £20 million

The money goes round in circles

If investors still needed convincing even after all of the above, **Note 17 – Investments in joint ventures** (above) should have piqued their interest further as to what on earth was going on.

This note claims that Amey agreed to supply £20 million of services in the future to J J Gallagher, a privately owned construction company. Then, following the 2001 year end, Amey agreed to invest £20 million in J J Gallagher. It looks as if the money Amey invested in J J Gallagher was going round in circles and ending up as sales in the books of Amey.

The asset write-downs reported in the 2002 Amey Annual Report as exceptional items should not have surprised anyone who had read the 2001 Amey Annual Report, or indeed who had taken an interest in how its joint venture to run trams between the London suburbs of Croydon and Wimbledon (on which few paid fares) was doing.

With debt already high, Amey's hand was forced when it needed further cash to buy back its £60 million interest in Tube Lines, a company that looked after the infrastructure of some of the London Underground network. Enter Ferrovial with a 32p bid for Amey and the cash so desperately required to buy back the Tube Lines jewel in the Amey crown. Amey is now owned by Ferrovial, a Spanish infrastructure company that specialises in transport.

Lesson

Significant increases in accrued income, prepayments and long-term receivables over the levels seen in the previous year was a slam dunk of what should have concerned any reader of the 2001 Amey Annual Report. Eric Tracey, the temporary finance director, was clearly not happy with the level of these assets and wrote down much of their value. As a matter of record, losses at Amey in 2002 were £129 million, but they rose to £224 million in 2003. However, the writing on the wall was already there in the 2001 Amey Annual Report for anyone who bothered to look.

Capita

HIGH QUALITY TO LOW QUALITY

Capita provides business process services and integrated support services, many for government organisations. For example, it runs the congestion charge for Transport for London. With a stock market valuation of £8.8 billion in 2015, Capita was once a stock market darling and seen as a high-quality company – but not any more. As with a number of outsourcing companies, a series of profit warnings have reduced expectations for the future. Shareholders have had to bail out the company in a £700 million rights issue and the dividend has been ditched for now.

Capita was floated on the USM (the forerunner of AIM) in 1989 at a paltry value of £8 million by its then finance director, Paul Pindar, a newly qualified but confident young chartered accountant and venture capitalist, and Rod Aldridge, who later resigned as Capita's chairman after it was revealed that he had lent the Labour Party £1 million. At its peak in 2015, Capita was worth billions and employed 75,000 people at 500 sites. The company had remarkable success feeding off the government's and industry's insatiable appetite at the time for outsourcing non-core activities to others, whilst concentrating on what they thought they did best.

Meanwhile, largely because of acquisitions, its borrowings rose, which meant important bank covenants needed watching. Prior to the share price collapse, which began in 2016, the preceding annual reports had shown a sharp decline in current asset quality which should have signalled that there was trouble ahead for Capita – the supposedly high-quality stock market darling.

First ever profit warnings

It was all going so well at Capita at the beginning of 2016. It continued to take advantage of the trend of outsourcing non-core functions like business processing and IT activities by both private companies and publicly owned organisations. The shares were highly rated too, trading on an expensive valuation – surprising really as more recently there had been an increasing tendency for Capita to focus on 'underlying profits' rather than actual reported profits when communicating with investors. In arriving at 'underlying profits', the company tended to exclude such items as: provisions on contracts that were not going so well; plant and equipment write-downs; professional fees; and losses on disposals of unwanted activities. All of which was done presumably in order to present the company's profits in a better light. Many would say that, as these types of costs occurred regularly, they should be included in 'underlying profits'. But there were others who did not take this view, which is why, despite all the classic warning signs, they chased the shares up and gave Capita such a high valuation.

Then in the second half of 2016, the company issued two profit warnings in quick succession. As you can see from the share price chart, the first came in late September 2016, driving

Capita shares hit twenty-year low

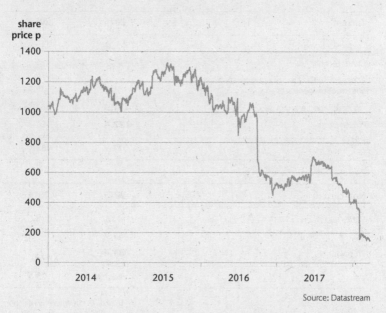

Source: Datastream

a London bus through market expectations for profit for the full year. Capita shares lost nearly 40% of their value in the following month. The company blamed delayed decision-making by clients; a slowdown generally with some outsourcing clients; and one-off costs incurred on the London congestion charge contract. In late 2016, Capita's IT services division was cited as a further problem. Original expectations for 'underlying profits' for 2016 were £615 million, but in the end only £475 million was reported. Actual reported profits were not much at all, at £75 million – less than a sixth of the so-called 'underlying profits'. In January 2018 Jonathan Lewis, from engineering project management company Amec Foster Wheeler, was appointed CEO, and he warned again

Note 18: Trade and other receivables, an extract, £m

Current	2015	2014
Trade receivables	412.4	449.5
Other receivables	21.3	22.0
Gross amounts due from customers on construction contracts	39.3	48.2
Accrued income	411.5	361.7
Prepayments	127.4	106.7
	1,011.9	988.1

Non-current	2015	2014
Other receivables	13.0	8.0
Accrued income	41.7	44.4
Prepayments	31.4	21.1
	86.1	73.5

Source: 2015 Capita Annual Report

Accrued income and prepayments = 56% of total trade and other receivables

that profits would be below even previously reduced expectations. Should investors have seen the profit warnings coming?

Since then Capita has suspended its dividend and the new CEO aims to reduce the spread of the company's activities so that there is more focus and less complexity. To refinance the company, £700 million has been raised through a discounted rights issue. In spite of being a company with clear financial risks, in 2018 the Ministry of Defence awarded Capita a £500 million contract to run the fire and rescue services on its bases.

Note 19: Trade and other receivables, an extract, £m

Current	2010	2009
Trade receivables	385.6	308.1
Other receivables	23.7	27.8
Gross amounts due from customers on construction contracts	20.3	25.4
Accrued income	**215.0**	168.4
Prepayments	**59.6**	47.2
	704.2	576.9

Non-current	2010	2009
Other receivables	25.4	20.3
Accrued income	**31.1**	35.4
Prepayments	**10.3**	6.1
	66.8	61.8

Source: 2010 Capita Annual Report

Accrued income and prepayments = 41% of total trade and other receivables

Warning signs

The warning signs in the 2015 Capita Annual Report, published a year before the share price collapsed, were in the quality of the assets on the balance sheet. It's worth remembering one maxim when analysing the accounts in a company's annual report: cash is fact, everything else is a matter of opinion. For auditors there are assets that are easy to value – such as cash – and assets that are not so easy to value – goodwill, for example, where they rely on management's assurances and forecasts – which are not so reliable.

As we already know, accrued income is another more difficult balance to audit and large balances in particular should be looked at carefully, as they can impact profits significantly.

In the 2015 Capita Annual Report, **Note 18 – Trade and other receivables** (see page 158) deserves particular scrutiny, as it is here that we can see that accrued income and prepayments had risen dramatically from five years previously, as shown in **Note 19 – Trade and other receivables** (see previous page) in the 2010 Capita Annual Report.

In 2010, accrued income and prepayments accounted for 41% of trade and other receivables; in 2015, this had risen to 56% – a 94% increase in value. In 2015, accrued income was nearly as large as trade receivables itself. This was an unusually big amount and another reason for further investigation.

It is worth remembering here how US companies show their current assets in their balance sheets. They are presented in order of liquidity, in other words the order in which they could be most easily converted into cash. So cash comes first, then marketable securities, trade receivables, inventory and finally prepayments and accrued income – or, to put it another way, in order of asset quality. When viewed like this, a rise in the value of lower quality assets should have been seen as an obvious warning sign that things at Capita were not as good as they used to be, indicating perhaps a less rigorous approach to asset determination and more risk in their recovery.

Lesson

The balance sheet is perhaps the most important part of a company's financial statements to investigate, as it is here that the bad news is often buried. However, it is often the case that insufficient attention is paid to the quality of the assets that comprise the balance sheet and how they have changed over time. Current assets clearly are not all the same and it strikes me that, had these been looked at more over time at Capita, the right questions would have been asked and many investors would have got out well before the share price started to fall.

In the analysis of a bank's assets, UK government bonds are considered to be good quality assets, whereas junk bonds – that is, loans to low credit scoring firms – are bad quality assets. And so it is with current assets – better to have cash or, failing that, invoiced trade receivables than prepayments or accrued income, as cash equivalents and invoiced trade receivables are usually more easily converted into cash. The dramatic rise in the accrued income balance at Capita, in particular, should have been a warning, as should the company's continued focus on 'underlying profits' which ignored the costs that were all taken into account when arriving at a company's actual profit. Sadly, Capita was not the only company that did this.

Carillion

A BUSY FOOL

Carillion was a busy company. It built part of Heathrow's Terminal 5, the Royal Opera House, the Liverpool FC stadium expansion and Union Station in Toronto. Because of these types of prestigious contracts, and importantly a number of acquisitions, sales advanced from £4.0 billion to a busy £5.2 billion over the ten years to 2016. But Carillion was also very foolish, because it is growth in earnings or profits over time, not sales, that are the key determinants to share price performance. While sales increased, earnings per share at Carillion were virtually static and debt rose significantly over those ten years. Needless to say, the value of one of the UK government's favourite construction and support services company fell to zero over virtually the same period – proving the old saying that sales are vanity and profit is sanity! A massive profit warning in mid 2017 did most of the damage, but Carillion's shares had been serial underperformers even before that. Although troubled companies often go into administration so that there is a more orderly wind-up of the business as assets and businesses are sold off, Carillion's circumstances were so dire in January 2018 that, having failed to secure further financing from its bankers, it was decided that there was no alternative but to put it into liquidation.

Born out of a demerger from the huge aggregates-to-construction company Tarmac in 1999, Carillion went on the acquisition trail, with key captures being John Mowlem (£350 million), Alfred McAlpine (£554 million) and Eaga (£298 million). What the Carillion board really wanted to buy were support services companies, so that they could add to the lucrative deals they already had to manage the UK's military bases and maintain the tracks for Network Rail. But every time the banks and shareholders allowed Carillion to open the cheque book, it was construction services they got more than they bargained for. Alfred McAlpine and Mowlem were testament to that. Meanwhile, Eaga, a renewable energy specialist and support services company, saw its raison d'être disappear almost as soon as it was acquired when the UK government cut subsidies for solar panels. In 2014, Carillion attempted its largest deal yet – a merger with another construction giant, Balfour Beatty, engineered perhaps to paper over the cracks that were already appearing. But this merger was swiftly rejected by the Balfour Beatty board of directors – as a result of which its shareholders will be sleeping more easily. Carillion's acquisition strategy was a disaster.

In 2017 it was construction services that were causing all the problems, for a whole host of reasons highlighted below, and Carillion announced a massive impairment provision of £845 million to cater for expected losses on four key challenging construction contracts, in particular: the Midland Metropolitan Hospital, Smethwick; the Royal Liverpool Hospital; the Aberdeen bypass; and a large contract in Doha, Qatar. There was also a £200 million provision thrown in for good measure to cover poor performing support service contracts. The share price reacted predictably and there were significant management changes at the top, with the chief executive, Richard Howson, departing hastily and the finance director, Zafar Khan, following shortly afterwards. The previous finance director, Richard Adam, had made his escape promptly at the end of 2016. The appointment of Keith Cochrane, of Weir Group fame, to take over on a temporary basis as chief executive was not enough to prevent Carillion from finally coming off the rails and going bust in January 2018.

A long list of issues identified ...

In the ten years to 2016, earnings per share at Carillion went nowhere but debt went up significantly. Following the realisation that there was in total a £1.0 billion provision required for the construction services and support services book, Keith Cochrane, the interim CEO, compiled a long list of issues that Carillion needed to address, shown in no particular order below:

- Contracts were too complex.
- There were too many layers of management – meaning too many people employed to do not much.
- There was a focus on the short term.
- Too much noisy data around meant that management could not see the wood for the trees.
- There was too much not-very-busy overhead.
- There were too many unprofitable contracts.
- Group profitability relied on one-offs such as PFI disposals.
- Mobilisation costs on new contracts were too high.

Going nowhere forever – and eventually off the rails

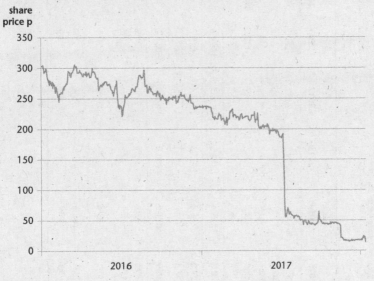

share price p

Source: Datastream

- There was too much bidding for contracts that were not profitable and often cash-flow negative for too long.
- There was a lack of accountability and professionalism.
- Contract execution was often third party dependent and difficult to control.
- Poor management of customer claims meant that reworks were destroying contract margins.

A damning list indeed … perhaps the only surprise is that Carillion did not go bust sooner – as many had expected.

Trade and other receivables, 2011–2016, £m

	2016	2015	2014	2013	2012	2011	change 2011–16
Trade receivables	229.5	253.1	242.1	219.7	236.1	282.7	−19%
Amounts owed on construction contracts	**614.5**	**386.8**	437.7	386.0	343.6	321.5	+91%
Other receivables	**749.5**	**550.1**	511.4	482.3	412.4	350.5	+114%
Amounts owed by joint ventures	59.9	59.6	128.7	108.8	107.7	128.5	−53%
Amounts owed under jointly controlled operations	10.6	21.2	5.5	15.5	8.9	11.4	−7%
Total receivables	1664.0	1270.8	1325.4	1212.3	1108.7	1094.6	+52%
Support services sales	3025.7	2727.0	2486.4	2537.8	2647.4	3019.0	0%
Construction services sales	2188.5	1859.9	1585.5	1543.1	1755.4	2032.2	+8%
Total sales	5214.2	4586.9	4071.9	4080.9	4402.8	5051.2	+3%
Trade receivables % of total	14%	20%	18%	18%	21%	26%	
Other receivables % of total	45%	43%	39%	40%	37%	32%	
Amounts owed on construction contracts % of total	37%	30%	33%	32%	31%	29%	
Other receivables and construction contracts % of total	82%	74%	72%	72%	68%	61%	
Time taken to pay Carillion in days	**112**	**95**	**107**	**97**	**82**	**69**	

Lower quality assets rising significantly

Invoiced receivables falling

Virtually no growth in 5 years

46% increase in lower quality receivables in 1 year

Customers increasingly slow to pay Carillion

Source: 2011–2016 Carillion Annual Reports

... but the warning signs had been there all along

Let's list these, too:

- Sometimes short sellers get it wrong, but it is a warning sign if there is a large short position in a company's shares – which there was with Carillion.

- Carillion had made a number of large acquisitions but they failed to deliver positive earnings progression.

- Debt was rising, and average debt for the period was always higher than that which was disclosed at the year end. Some debt was mysteriously hidden in 'other creditors' in the balance sheet. This was the debt arising from the operation of the early payment facility that allowed subcontractors to be paid for a fee.

- The pension deficit was growing quickly.

But the real clue to the worsening of the trading position at Carillion was the deterioration in its balance sheet quality, especially in the current assets. This had been evident in recent Carillion annual reports, in particular in 2016.

Let's make the following points. Even though sales just about rose over the five years before Carillion went bust, invoiced amounts shown in trade receivables were falling. Trade receivables – that is, invoiced amounts for work already done – are regarded as good quality current assets and it is best to have these rising in line with sales. However, poorer quality current assets were rising – and these included balances that were much more difficult for KPMG, Carillion's Birmingham-based auditor, to verify. This would have involved getting satisfactory and credible management assurances on amounts owed on, for example, complicated hospital contracts and the Aberdeen bypass. Meanwhile, other receivables, which included prepayments and accrued income, rose a staggering 114% over the five years to 2016 against a sales rise of only 3% over the same period.

There were clearly very large changes going on in the accounting at Carillion – or perhaps the way it carried out its business – which were not positive. Amounts owed on construction contracts rose in the period by 91%, even though sales for construction only rose by 8% in the same period. These amounts, which included subjective profits, are also difficult to substantiate for auditors. However, a simple analysis of the annual reports told us that Carillion was taking longer to get paid by its customers, indicating perhaps that they were quarrelling with the company about how much they owed. We now know that this was the case. All in all, the lower quality assets such as amounts owed on construction projects and prepayments were making up a greater and greater proportion of current assets – a worrying sign which should have indicated that something was going to give. Which of course it did!

In mid 2017 Carillion broke the news that a £1 billion provision on outstanding construction and support services contracts was required. Only just over three months earlier, on 1 March 2017, the auditors had signed off that these contracts and receivables were worth £1.6 billion. Now, apparently, they were worth 60% less and needed adjusting by £1 billion. How could the situation have changed so quickly? Following the appointment of a liquidator in January 2018, the accountancy profession's regulator, the FRC, announced that it was investigating Richard Adam and Zafar Khan, the two former finance directors, as well as the audit of Carillion from 2014 to 2017 by the company's auditor, KPMG.

In particular contract accounting, reverse factoring, pensions, goodwill and going concern are being investigated. That there might be problems with some of these issues was clear from the 2016 Carillion Annual Report and indeed earlier ones. KPMG says that it conducted the audits of Carillion 'appropriately and responsibly' and that it uncovered the shortfalls in the company's finances in summer 2017.

Lesson

The cash required to pay off the mushrooming debt at Carillion was included in trade receivables, accruals of income and amounts owed to them for construction contracts. Assessing their collectability is an important piece of analysis. The analysis on page 148 shows that at Carillion lower quality current assets were growing fast, and therefore paying down the debt was going to be more difficult – this was enough of a warning sign that its shares should have been avoided. This was particularly the case in 2016, when sales grew by 14% but the amounts owed to Carillion on construction projects and other receivables grew by 46%. That they were heavily out of line with sales growth should have indicated that there were likely to be problems in their recoverability – which of course there were.

Aston Martin Lagonda

STUFFED

W hy use one investment bank to raise £1 billion when you can use twelve? The big bosses at the bulge bracket bank Morgan Stanley in New York must have been hopping up and down when they discovered their European underlings were among the few bankers to miss out on the perceived prestigious flotation on the London Stock Exchange (LSE) of luxury car maker Aston Martin Lagonda (AML) in 2018. Perhaps they thought the UK's remaining luxury car maker was just too highly valued by twelve of their competitors and they simply wanted to duck this IPO. If so, they were right. It was after all valued pretty much in line with the Prancing Horse – Ferrari, the Italian manufacturer of supercars, and for some that was a bit rich as Aston Martin had gone bust 007 times in its not so illustrious past. A bit of a car crash then in terms of its corporate history, but Aston Martin had often been bailed out by rich enthusiasts who no doubt regarded it as one of their playthings.

AML came to the market in 2018 valued at £4.3 billion which was 56 times its most recent reported profits. Reassuringly expensive some would say. Others might point to the losses racked up in the years before the flotation of the company on the LSE; the high levels of debt (over £610 million) that remained with the company in spite of the fundraising that only satisfied those investors wanting to sell some of their shares; the extended credit the company appeared to be taking from its suppliers; and the high deferred development costs (£570 million).

As recently as 2016 AML had posted losses of £148 million but in 2017 a profit of £77 million was reported. Andy Palmer, recruited from Nissan in 2014, had remarkably turned losses into profits and now the patient Kuwaiti and Italian investors wanted to check out of 25% of their holdings. So, it was decided to float the company, which allowed them to sell some of their shares and provide liquidity to others who may wish to trade in them.

Aston Martin, established in 1913, is a quintessentially British motor brand often associated with the fictional MI6 Secret Service agent James Bond. In all, in its history up to the flotation, it had manufactured just 60,000 cars and is currently producing over 6,000 each year. In some years, however, it manufactured as few as 200 cars and it is remarkable that the marque survived those lean times. Of course, it might not have survived at all but, just at the right time, it had a stroke of luck. Sir William Lyons, then the managing director of Jaguar Cars, apparently could not find two spare E-types for Albert Broccoli to use in the James Bond films back in the day. So in 1965 he turned to Aston Martin for the film 'Goldfinger' and the rest, as they say, is history.

New management under Andy Palmer, who was once described by an Italian investor as a British Midlands industrialist merged with a Japanese perfectionist, turned things round very quickly at AML. The change was due to the execution of his

'Second Century Plan' which involved stabilising the company, strengthening its core and expanding its portfolio of products. He introduced a three-pillar product strategy that included luxury sedans, sports cars and SUVs in order to take the Aston Martin and Lagonda brands to a wider global market place. The plan was to launch a new core model each year with the range being enhanced by special editions and derivatives.

The aim was to steer the business in the direction of the increasing number of high net worth individuals, especially in China and other parts of Asia. This target market was expected to grow at a rate of 7% per annum globally. AML also had its sights set on increasing the appeal of its cars among women and younger drivers. Previously, AML had targeted only men of a certain age. In order to cope with the expected demand, there were plans to expand the number of dealers and production. Its worldwide network of dealers was to increase from 160 to 200 with the growth mainly overseas. The medium-term target for annual production volumes was 14,000 and to help achieve this a new factory was established in St Athan, Wales, for the future production and launch of SUVs in 2020. Importantly, AML was developing hybrid and electric cars and the intention is that Lagonda will be the world's first all-electric luxury automotive brand.

Investors taken for a ride

AML shares were floated in October 2018 and the newly listed company announced its maiden results in February 2019. After being floated at a price of £19, the shares closed at just over £18 on the first day of trading – not a great start to its life as a public company. The share price has never been close to £19 since and

One-way traffic – downhill

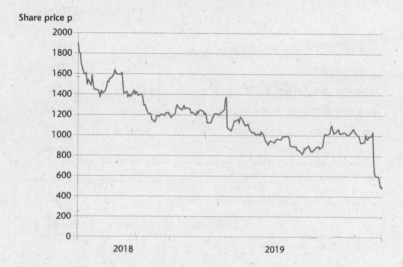

Share price p

Source: Datastream

the shares look friendless, having fallen to below £5 in August 2019.

The 2018 preliminary results steered one to figures that were all good – sales up 25% at £1.1 billion, with excellent advance orders in Asia and the US, and adjusted operating profits were 18% better at £147 million. But a look under the bonnet of the 2018 preliminary results revealed other numbers that were not so good. There was the £61 million of incentives to AML management, the £62 million spent on redeeming the preference shares, and the £13 million paid to the bankers who did such a great job on the IPO. It all added up to a loss before tax of £68 million for 2018.

And then there was the massive increase in receivables due

Preliminary results for the 12 months ended, an extract, £m

	31 Dec 2017	31 Dec 2018
Revenue	876.0	1,096.5
Trade receivables	72.0	191.5
Trade receivable turnover period	30 days	64 days
Increase in average credit period		+113%
Approx. number of cars at dealers[a]	452	1,204
Increase in amounts owed by dealers		+166%

Source: 2008 Aston Martin Lagonda Annual Report

a Assuming average sales price of cars was £159,000.

Dealers taking extended credit   *Channel stuffing*

from the 160 dealers. So, whilst sales grew by an impressive 25% in the period, the amounts owed by the AML dealer network to the company rose by 166% to £191.5 million and on average in 2018 the dealers were taking 64 days to pay compared with 30 days on average in 2017 – see **Prelimary results for the 12 months ended** (above). Put this another way: at the end of 2018, AML's dealers had around 1200 cars in the distribution channel compared with around 450 cars only a year earlier. The distribution channel had taken quite a stuffing it seems. The stuffing endured into 2019. For the interim results for the six months ended June 2019, AML continued to give the same broad level of credit they gave to their dealers in 2018 to encourage them to take more cars and whilst retail sales advanced, wholesale sales were disappointing. This was hardly surprising as perhaps for some dealers they just did not have the space to store all those new Valkyries and Superleggeras.

This meant that there was a large increase in inventories at AML with the consequence of rising debt. No wonder it was now the debt levels that also troubled investors.

But you did not have to wait until the preliminary results for 2018 or the following interim results, to realise that something had changed in the distribution channel. It was obvious to anyone who bothered to look at the helpful IPO prospectus published before the shares were listed on the LSE.

The signs in the prospectus

The 2018 AML prospectus included trading for the six months ended 30 June 2017 and for the six months ended 30 June 2018

Historical financial information, an extract, £m

	31 Dec 2017 (12 months)	30 June 2017 (6 months)	30 June 2018 (6 months)
Revenue	876.0	410.3	444.9
Trade receivables	72.0	76.4[a]	114.5
Trade receivable turnover period	30 days	34 days	47 days
Increase in average credit period			+38%
Approx. number of cars at dealers[b]	452	480	720
Estimated increase in cars at dealers			+50%

Source: 2018 Aston Martin Lagonda Prospectus

a Trade and other receivables is not given in the 2018 Aston Martin Lagonda prospectus but it is calculated using data from the consolidated statement of cash flows for the six months ended 30 June 2017 and the trade receivables at 31 December 2016.
b Assuming average sale price of cars was £159,000.

Channel stuffing

Dealers taking extended credit

and a balance sheet at that date. Sadly, it did not publish a balance sheet at 30 June 2017 which would have included an amount for what was owed by the dealer network to AML, but we can calculate this number using other information in the prospectus. The analysis in **Historical financial information** (previous page) shows that the amounts owed by the dealers to AML rose by 50% in the year to 30 June 2018 to £114.5 million and that the dealers were taking on average 47 days to pay as against on average 34 days in the six months to 30 June 2017. In the context of a mere 8% rise in sales in the six month period to 30 June 2018 these large increases in amounts owed by dealers is significant. There is a limit to how much inventory of prestigious Aston Martin Lagonda cars a distribution channel can take, especially in view of the imminent arrival of new designs, including the Superleggera Volante, Vantage AMR, DB4 GT Zagato and importantly the DBX, Aston Martin's first SUV.

Lesson

It is always worth giving an IPO prospectus a thorough investigation ahead of deciding whether to invest in a company listing its shares on a stock exchange for the first time. There is more detail in a prospectus than in an annual report and therefore it can provide more helpful information on which to base your decision. And so it was for AML.

It is in the interests of a company to present its financial information in the most beneficial manner so that the highest valuation is attached to the value of the company. The very significant growth in the amounts owed by the dealer network to AML was worthy of investigation in view of the much slower growth in sales in the period leading up to the flotation of the company. The high amounts owed by the dealer network may raise revenue recognition issues and also raised questions about the distributors' ability to take more inventory from AML, especially in view of the new models in the pipeline.

PART 7

Crunch

THERE IS NO IGNORING BAD DEBTS

Anyone can lend money. It's getting it back that is difficult. The chairmen of Northern Rock and Cattles, both providers of finance to consumers, said before their share prices collapsed to nothing that their businesses were doing well. Apparently the 'success' of Cattles before its transformation from livestock to dead stock in April 2009 was, among other things, due to 'robust credit quality'. In similar vein, the chairman of Northern Rock said that his company had a 'strategy of using … credit quality to reward both shareholders and customers'. Nothing could have been further from the truth for Cattles: a review undertaken by the new management team installed in 2009 revealed that in 2007 the company had not in fact made the reported profit of £165 million but a loss of £96 million. The original loan or bad debt provision was totally inadequate.

Northern Rock, a mortgage provider, had similar issues and a cursory look at its balance sheet would have revealed that its own loan or bad debt provision was totally inadequate, too. If you had noticed this as an investor you may have ditched the shares way before the wholesale banking market froze in September 2008 – and with it Northern Rock's ability to finance itself and its growth. You see, bad debts matter.

Although Northern Rock grew its loan book to customers in 2006 by 23% to nearly £85 billion, its bad debt provision hardly moved. It was pretty much the same story at Cattles, where as a percentage of outstanding loans the provision for bad debts actually fell in 2007 over the previous year, even though the loans outstanding had risen by 38%. These are anomalies, to say the least, which should have been grounds to avoid both companies' shares.

For lending companies such as Cattles and Northern Rock, the loan loss or bad debt provision that needs to be calculated so that the value of the outstanding loans is correctly stated in the balance sheet is the key number for an auditor to get right. This requires a great deal of judgement. Profits depend on it.

In the days of Cattles and Northern Rock, provisioning would have centred around the age analysis of the loans and some general provisioning, with the audit of the figure arrived at involving a great deal of discussion with management to form an opinion of its adequacy. Back then, a great deal of subjectivity would have been applied, whereas now a more objective approach is employed. If there is objective evidence that a group of financial assets are impaired, then this must be recognised in the income statement. The loss is the difference between the carrying value and the present value of the expected cash flows discounted at the effective interest rate, which is usually the company's cost of capital. Current financial reporting standards are more proscriptive as to how loan losses and bad debt provisions are calculated, so the subjectivity that caused the woeful under-provisioning and overstatement of profits in these two money lenders is less likely to be repeated.

Northern Rock

BUILT ON SAND NOT GRANITE

The last time there was a run on a British bank prior to Northern Rock was in 1866. It was the 'banker's banker' Overend, Gurney and Company that found itself in trouble then, and depositors laid siege to the head office at 65 Lombard Street, London. The company had changed its business model, having moved from discounting bills of exchange to making increasingly risky loans. There were no financial regulators like the FCA and PRA to help in those days. Following loan write-offs and with no support from the Bank of England, it was unable to return cash to its depositors. Panic set in outside its offices not just in London but in Liverpool, Manchester, Norwich, Derby and Bristol. Sounds familiar, doesn't it?

Northern Rock came from humble beginnings. It started life as a building society which demutualised and listed on the London Stock Exchange in October 1997 to become the UK's fourth largest bank for all sorts of lending. It played a large part in the life of the north-east of England, in particular contributing some

£230 million to local charitable causes. It sponsored Newcastle United Football Club. It employed nearly 6,000 full and part-time staff, and from 2004 was chaired by Matt Ridley, a journalist and writer, who had joined the board in 1994, not long after his father, Viscount Ridley, had stepped down. Keeping it in the family did not help at Northern Rock. In the five years up to its demise in 2007 it had grown its assets at a compound growth rate of 25%, while its profits had grown at a rate of 18% per annum. At its peak share price of £12.51 Northern Rock was worth over £6 billion. In the first half of 2007 it was the largest mortgage lender in the country. Northern Rock was the pride of the Geordie nation.

But 141 years after Overend, Gurney and Company collapsed, the panic played out again outside Northern Rock's Moorgate offices and across the country, especially in the north-east, when, on 14 September 2007, it asked the Bank of England for financial support. The run on Northern Rock had begun.

Sand not granite

Instead of using sticky customer deposits to fund its lending growth, Northern Rock had resorted to an entirely different funding model that required other banks to lend to it for short periods. It also relied on the sale of mortgage-backed securities through a special purpose vehicle (SPV) called Granite. But this novel funding strategy did not function when the wholesale banking market (that is, lending by one bank to another) stopped dealing with Northern Rock and the liquidity in mortgage-backed securities dried up. It is always a liquidity trigger that starts a run on a bank and Northern Rock was no exception. Northern Rock was not built on the granite of deposits from a large number of small savers but mainly on the sand of the wholesale banking market, a much more fickle source of capital. Because of this weakness, Northern Rock failed more dramatically than other banks in the financial crisis.

With these sources of funding gone for Northern Rock, it was up to the UK Treasury to take up the slack, which it did, pumping in £37 billion over time to keep it afloat, allowing depositors to remove their cash and funding the business generally. Of course shareholders have got nothing back, but there were clear signs in the 2006 Northern Rock Annual Report that this was a risky share to own – as the share price graph opposite illustrates.

For those in the know, and for those who understood the Northern Rock business model, the panic should have set in a month before its government bail-out, when liquidity in US sub-prime mortgage securities had dried up and the French bank BNP Paribas froze withdrawals on funds with exposure to US mortgage-backed securities. Northern Rock partly relied upon the sale of similar UK mortgage-backed securities to finance its growth through Granite, which had been magically turning an expected flow of cash from long-term mortgages over twenty-five years into cash today for the Northern Rock team to lend out again to potential home buyers to keep profits rocking and rolling. An important part of Northern Rock's financing model was now shattered as liquidity in the secondary market for mortgage-backed securities dried up. The game was up.

On top of this, for much of 2007 Northern Rock was finding it difficult to borrow in the wholesale banking market, with other banks increasingly reluctant to lend to it because of its perceived weak loan book. Other banks, which may have been prepared to lend short term to Northern Rock, saw the 125% loans to value

Shares hit the rocks

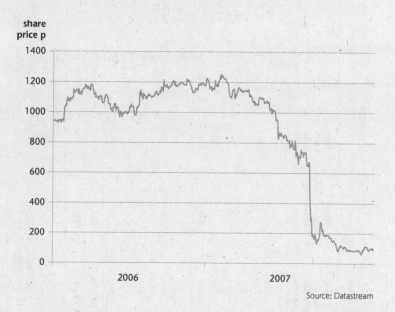

Source: Datastream

mortgages it was offering customers as unduly risky – and they were right.

Ironically, whilst its failure was there for all to see in 2007 as depositors scrambled to take their cash out and shareholders were left with nothing, as of today the government looks like it has pretty much recovered all that it lent to Northern Rock. Some would say that is not fair but, as any shareholder should know, they are the last in the pecking order when it comes to insolvencies.

Current ratio

As any fresh-faced newly qualified accountant will tell you, there are a number of ways that one can test the solvency of a company.

Note 37: Financial risk management, an extract, £m

The table below analyses the Group's assets and liabilities into relevant maturity groupings based on the remaining period at balance sheet date to contractual maturity date. Amounts shown in respect of loans and advances to customers include fair value adjustments of portfolio hedging.

2006	Within 3 months	After 3 months but within 6 months	After 6 months but within 1 year	After 1 year but within 5 years	After 5 years	Total
Assets						
Cash and balances with central banks	876.3	—	—	—	79.7	956.0
Derivative financial instruments	100.8	83.5	84.1	471.6	131.3	871.3
Loans and advances to banks	5,483.8	122.5	15.0	—	—	5,621.3
Loans and advances to customers	900.1	593.3	1,175.6	11,319.8	72,372.9	86,361.7
Investment securities	864.6	139.5	587.3	1,947.4	3,091.6	6,630.4
Other assets	110.3	12.1	23.1	108.4	316.0	569.9
Total assets	**8,335.9**	**950.9**	**1,885.1**	**13,847.2**	**75,991.5**	**101,010.6**
Liabilities						
Deposits by banks	1,823.8	88.4	53.0	137.3	33.7	2,136.2
Customer accounts	19,598.5	1,680.6	3,689.7	1,898.8	—	**26,867.6**
Derivative financial instruments	485.1	143.9	355.6	1,111.3	296.6	2,392.5
Debt securities in issue	10,989.7	621.4	1,430.0	7,000.2	44,253.0	64,294.3
Subordinated liabilities	—	—	—	—	762.4	762.4
Tier one notes	—	—	—	—	209.4	209.4
Other liabilities	803.6	191.1	93.0	16.0	33.9	1,137.6
Total liabilities	**33,700.7**	**2,725.4**	**5,621.3**	**10,163.6**	**45,589.0**	**97,800.0**
Net liquidity gap	(25,364.8)	(1,774.5)	(3,736.2)	3,683.6	30,402.5	3,210.6

Source: 2006 Northern Rock Annual Report

Deposits by sticky retail customers only 27% of funding

Liquidity gap over 1 year £30.8 billion

$$\frac{Current\ assets}{Current\ liabilities} = \frac{11,171}{42,047} = 0.27$$

One way is to calculate the current ratio – a fundamental liquidity ratio that measures the ability of companies (including banks, by the way) to repay current liabilities with current assets. It's quite simple, really. For Northern Rock one divides current assets that can be converted into cash within twelve months, such as loans to other banks and customers, by current liabilities such as deposits by customers and loans from other banks that are repayable within twelve months. The rule of thumb for normal companies is that this number should be over 1.0, meaning that the company is not facing a liquidity problem. **Note 37 – Financial risk management** (opposite) in the 2006 Northern Rock Annual Report shows that its current ratio was 0.27, indicating that on a bog standard analysis there was a solvency issue. It even highlights this for anyone to see as a 'liquidity gap'.

Now, there will be some readers jumping up and down saying that a bank always borrows short and lends long. Agreed! But Northern Rock was doing this at an extreme level, as it was failing to attract large numbers of 'sticky' (that is, reliable and long-lasting) retail customer deposits and instead was relying on a handful of banks to support its ambitious growth plan. In 2006, just before the run on the bank, only 27% of Northern Rock's external funding came from sticky retail customer deposits. Contrast this with Virgin Money today, the business that acquired Northern Rock from the UK government. It has 85% of its outside funding from sticky retail customer deposits and sources virtually nothing from the wholesale banking market – a much more solvent position. Of the many criticisms that can be levelled at the management of Northern Rock, one major one is that it should have pursued its very ambitious growth plans by growing its customer deposit account business.

An impaired impairment

In 2006 Northern Rock increased its loan book to customers by 23% to £86.4 billion. That's quite a lot. It is curious then that the impairment provision in **Note 8 – Impairment losses on loans and advances** (opposite) in the 2006 Northern Rock Annual Report moved up by only 1%. This was a sure sign that the impairment provisioning was impaired. What could possibly have caused the loan book to be of better quality in 2006 than it was in 2005? Northern Rock's finance director Dave Jones, deputy chief executive David Barker and Richard Barclay, a credit officer there, were subsequently fined by the FSA for misreporting mortgage arrears and repossessions. All three also had severe work restrictions placed on them. But let's be clear, Northern Rock did not go bust because of an impaired impairment provision on its loan book. This was just systematic of the problems there – though it was a good enough reason in itself to avoid the shares.

The 2006 Northern Rock Annual Report showed that an investment in its shares did not come without risk, as it relied on the goodwill of other banks. But even the regulator at the time, the FSA, admitted failings in its supervision of this 'high-impact firm'. Most catastrophically, it failed to spot the basic weakness in the bank's business model that it was becoming increasingly dependent on interbank lending, the extent of which was itself dependent on the lenders being happy with what kind of lending Northern Rock was doing – and 125% mortgages were not everyone's pint of Newcastle Brown at the time, it would appear.

Note 8: Impairment losses on loans and advances, an extract, £m

	On advances secured on residential property	On other secured advances	On unsecured loans	Total
At 1 January 2006	32.5	4.7	87.1	**124.3**
Income statement:				
Increase in allowance during the year net of recoveries	6.4	2.2	72.6	81.2
Amount written off during the year	(13.8)	–	(69.0)	(82.8)
Discount unwind	1.1	0.5	1.7	3.3
At 31 December 2006	26.2	7.4	92.4	**126.0**

Source: 2006 Northern Rock Annual Report

> *Virtually no change to impairment provision in spite of loans and advances rising by 23% to £86.4 billion in 2006*

Lesson

Whilst the use of quite elementary financial analysis such as current ratios can be too simplistic for a complicated lending business like Northern Rock, its use here would have highlighted that there were issues that were probably being glossed over by management. And however you look at it, having a liquidity gap of some £30.8 billion should not have been dismissed out of hand by so many. It was a serious warning sign. The FSA monitored independent investment banking analysts' recommendations generally in the period up to the financial crisis, and in its report on its own supervision of Northern Rock it notes that, prior to the run, 'market analysts were generally bullish about Northern Rock and its strategy'.

This analysis showed that 'analysts were more positive about the prospects of Northern Rock's share price than those of a number of other retail banks'. The analyst at Credit Suisse is credited by the FSA as the only long-term bear of Northern Rock, but his negative view was not supported by the actual reasons the bank went bust. Most commentators, including the regulator, it would appear, were happy with a funding strategy that relied on the wholesale banking market. But a simple current ratio analysis would have put them right – or at least identified issues which showed that Northern Rock's funding was too polarised and too risky. Oh, and the impairment provision on loans was clearly impaired – reason enough in itself to avoid the shares.

Cattles

LIVESTOCK TO DEAD STOCK

Some £1.3 billion of shareholder value was lost when Cattles shares were suspended in 2009. There was a cosy group of accountants and bankers on the board of the company, but even they could not stop the free fall in the value of shares of this doorstep lender to the financially challenged. Founded by Joseph Cattle as a drapery shop in Hull in 1927, Cattles diversified into lending small amounts of money, which were repaid weekly at the doorstep following a visit by one of an army of company agents – very often from the local community and well known to the borrowing families. 'We're like the man from the Pru, coming round to collect for something families otherwise couldn't afford,' said Cattles' former chief executive Sean Mahon reassuringly once. There will be many Cattles shareholders who will have wished it had been the man from the Pru they had invested in. Sean Mahon had been the bouncy, broad and bulky rugby-playing boss of Cattles – and interestingly a chartered accountant and former partner at the company's auditors – until he retired in 2007 to take up this new position. But actually his analogy with the man from the Pru was not strictly accurate: it was mostly women, not men, who did the debt collecting on the doorstep for Cattles.

If Cattles had stuck to the doorstep lending of small amounts of money with adequate controls in place and the loans had continued to be collected by the matriarchs of the community, then perhaps the company would still be thriving today. Instead, it moved to monthly repayments via direct debits, car finance and small business loans. In doing so, it failed to control its growth. Cattles' life as a publicly listed FTSE 250 company ended in 2009. Joseph Cattle, who was by all accounts a good and generous man, must have turned in his grave.

The auditors who failed to pick up the lack of an adequate impairment of the loan book at Welcome Finance, the key operating company at Cattles, settled out of court with the company's creditors for their negligent work. They were also fined £2.3 million by the accountancy watchdog, the FRC. Whatever representations the company's management made to the auditors about the quality of the loan book, common sense alone should have told them that the aggressive lending that Cattles was engaged in must be accompanied by a commensurate increase in the loan loss provision. In addition, the finance director of Cattles, James Corr, and two of his colleagues were fined by the FSA and banned from carrying out any functions in relation to FSA-regulated activities. From its peak share price of 404p, Cattles' fall from grace resulted in very significant losses for shareholders which made the fines levied by the regulators on Corr and his colleagues look pitifully small. But the 2007 Cattles Annual Report should have provided more than a warning prod for any potential or existing investor.

What growth, credit quality and efficiency?

Norman Broadhurst's Chairman's Statement, made up barely a third of a page of the 2007 Cattles Annual Report. It portrayed in an effortless, nonchalant, why-did-he-bother kind of way how the success of Cattles was due to 'disciplined **lending growth**, robust **credit quality** and improving operational and financial **efficiency**'. Interesting that a few months earlier another chairman, only a hundred miles further north, had said virtually the same thing. His company had had another excellent year, too, apparently and 'our strategy of using **growth**, cost **efficiency** and **credit quality** to reward both shareholders and customers continues to run well'. That chairman was Matt Ridley of Northern Rock.

A year later, in the 2008 Cattles Annual Report, Margaret Young, the company's newly appointed chairman, was having to explain in three full pages what had really happened in 2007: there was clearly no disciplined lending growth at all; credit quality was far from robust; and there was no operational and financial efficiency whatsoever. The original 2007 Cattles Annual Report had declared an advance in the profits from lending money of 25% to £165 million, but after the review by the new management team, this had been adjusted to a loss of £96 million.

In 2007 aggressive targets at Cattles pushed lending to customers at the important Welcome Finance division to £1.4 billion, an advance of 42% over the previous year. The problem was that there was a breakdown in internal controls and loans were made to poorer credit risks. The profits originally reported for 2007 failed to reflect that. Although the volumes of advances to customers had risen dramatically, many of these new clients were not able to pay their loans back – and the original

Dead stock

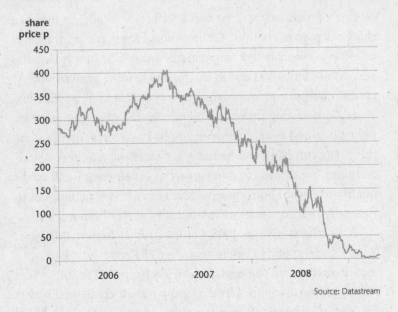

Source: Datastream

impairment provision for these loans was woefully inadequate. As a result of this loss of control, there was plenty of change at the top. Six senior executives, who had been suspended pending the results of the forensic review, were fired with immediate effect following the review; the group risk and treasury director departed; and both the chairman and the chief executive fell on their swords. It was up to a banker, Margaret Young, to clear up the mess.

Whilst it turned out that 2007 was a dreadful year for Cattles, 2008 was even worse – with losses reported of £745 million. Now, on a loan book of £2.8 billion (as reported originally at the end of 2007), that takes some doing. This magnitude of loss caused banking covenants to be breached and in April 2009 the shares were suspended. Shareholders got nothing back.

Impaired impairments

The warning signs in the 2007 Cattles Annual Report were poor cash flow from the outstanding loans and the fact that the impairment provision on these loans was increasingly being reduced and therefore becoming more inadequate. It was only a matter of time before it would become clear that the actual bad debts were substantially greater than allowed for in the accounts. This is what Margaret Young had to get to grips with.

Cattles bragged about how much Welcome Finance lent in 2006 and 2007. Knowing the loans outstanding at the year end, we can easily calculate the cash paid back to Cattles by the borrowers – and it doesn't look good. The analysis of loans outstanding is shown below. In 2007 new loans rose by 43%, so that by the year end the loans outstanding were up 38%. Given that Cattles customers paid back only 18% more in 2007 than they did in 2006, it was clear that

Analysis of loans outstanding, £m

	2007	2006	change
Welcome Finance loans at beginning of year	1,820	1,439	26%
New loans made	1,408	988	43%
Repayments made by customers	717	607	18%
Welcome Finance loans at end of year	2,511	1,820	38%

Source: 2006 and 2007 Cattles Annual Reports

Repayments not keeping pace with loan growth

Financial review Figure 7: Loans and receivables, £m

> Welcome Finance loans increased by 38% but arrears % fell

	2007	2006	Growth %
Welcome Finance	2,511	1,820	37.9
Shopacheck	101	114	(10.9)
Welcome Financial Services	2,612	1,934	35.0
The Lewis Group	133	91	46.0
Cattles Invoice Finance	99	80	23.9
Group	2,844	2,105	35.1

Financial review Figure 8: Welcome Finance instalment arrears, %

	2007	2006	2005
Traditional measure[1]	7.0	7.4	7.6
IFRS 7 basis			
Up to date	70.8	70.9	71.1
In arrears[2]	29.2	29.1	28.9
	100.0	100.0	100.0
In arrears			
Past due but not impaired	14.9	11.9	8.9
Impaired	14.3	17.2	20.0
	29.2	29.1	28.9

Source: 2007 Cattles Annual Report

Definitions
[1] Overdue instalments as a % of closing receivables
[2] Customer balances in arrears as a % of closing receivables

> Welcome Finance loans % in arrears but not impaired rose significantly

> Welcome Finance loans in arrears and impaired fell from 20% to 14% of loans

the credit risk was on the up. So why, then, was there no commensurate increase in the loan loss provision in 2007?

The adoption by Cattles in 2007 of IFRS 7 – Financial Instruments: Disclosures also tells us that clients were not paying back loans as quickly as they had been (see **Financial Reviews Figure** 7 and **Figure 8** opposite). This is hardly surprising, as the company's aggressive lending in 2007 would have certainly meant that the low-hanging fruit of good credit risk customers were becoming exhausted and new loans would need to find homes with an altogether different population of much riskier customers. Surprising, then, that in spite of the loan book rising by 38% at Welcome Finance in 2007, overdue instalments as a percentage of closing loans actually fell from 7.4% to 7.0%.

The IFRS 7 disclosures tell an additional story. They show that loans that were in arrears but were not being impaired had risen from 8.9% in 2005 to 14.9% in 2007. The impairment provision level at Welcome Finance fell from 20.0% of the loan book in 2005 to 14.3% in 2007. These changes would have had a considerable effect on profits and were a clear indication that less prudent accounting principles were being applied. The impairment provision of a loan book is the most important audit work, and large movements like this should have required diligent checking as they influence profits significantly. The loan loss provision or impairment provision of the group fell from 15% of gross loans in 2005 to 12% in 2007. If it had remained at 15% in 2007, reported profits at Cattles would have been nearly £100 million less – but that wouldn't do, would it?

Lesson

It's the big numbers that matter with specialist lenders, especially for companies like Cattles, which had aspirations to become a bank. Fortunately for all of us, it never got a banking licence. Its loan book was growing fast, but the loan loss provision was not keeping up. The loan book was the biggest number in the balance sheet and its value was dependent on the loan loss provision, which was itself one of the main determinants of profits. Seeing the loan loss provision fall as a percentage of gross loans, especially as cash repayments from borrowers was lagging the growth in the loan book, should have been enough of a steer for investors in Cattles to stampede for the exit.

PART 8

Too cosy for comfort

RELATED PARTY TRANSACTIONS

Related party transactions are rarely a serious issue with UK listed companies, not least because everyone from directors and shareholders to the auditors of UK public companies take a dim view of them. But if and when they are disclosed, it is always worth looking to see if they give cause for thought. The two companies featured in this section did not collapse because of related party transactions, but their disclosure in the companies' annual reports should have been enough of a distinct warning sign to show that sufficiently rigorous standards of governance were probably not being adhered to.

One of the most infamous recent related party incidents involved Asia Resource Minerals (formerly known as Bumi, an Indonesia coal miner and brainchild of Nathaniel Rothschild), which was a spectacular disaster. In 2015 the FCA fined the company a meagre £4.6 million for failing to report three related party transactions, one of which had a value of $225 million. At their peak, Bumi shares were worth £14 but, following the related party revelations and the failure to comply with the listing rules of the London Stock Exchange, the failure of the company to file an annual report and the suspension of its shares, investors agreed a bid for the company at just 56p. Related party transactions can have quite an effect, it seems.

IAS 24 – Related Party Disclosures insists on disclosures about transactions and outstanding balances with a company's related parties, thus allowing investors to consider the possibility that the company's financial position and results may have been affected by related party transactions.

Related parties can be persons and/or entities. Typically, a person or a close member of that person's family is related to a reporting entity if he or she has control over that entity, has significant influence over that entity, or is a member of key management of that entity.

An entity is related to a reporting entity if it is a member of the same group, or is an associate or joint venture of the other entity. Clearly if an associate of an entity does business with a joint venture of the same entity, then these are related parties, too.

There is nothing wrong with putting the family first in the right context. Blood is thicker than water, after all. But all shareholders in a company – family or not – are entitled to be treated equally.

Healthcare Locums

MULTIPLE TRAUMA

Within a year of Healthcare Locums hitting its peak share price at the beginning of 2010, its shares had been suspended and the company was virtually worthless. For the company's founder and chief executive, Kate Bleasdale, a former nurse who had once sung in an Abba tribute band which I'm guessing included in its repertoire 'The Winner Takes It All', this was the moment when she lost it all.

Kate Bleasdale set up Healthcare Locums in 2003 to supply healthcare professionals and social workers in both the public and private sectors. Some eight years later, Healthcare Locums' shares were suspended and the company was virtually worthless as a result of numerous accounting irregularities being discovered. Losses of £56 million were reported in 2011 as the accounts were adjusted for errors and a change in accounting policies. The company is now barely profitable and exists to all intents and purposes solely in order to service its debt and repay its financiers. But any investors who took the trouble to look could have seen from the 2009 Healthcare Locums Annual Report that all was not well and cashed in while the share price was riding high.

Polytraumas

Let's pretend to be a forensic pathologist and look at Healthcare Locums, the provider of healthcare specialists, as if it were a cadaver. The post mortem would say that it suffered death by a thousand cuts – that is, multiple traumas or polytraumas, perhaps none of which would have proven fatal by themselves, but together they were.

A forensic accountant who dissected the 2009 Healthcare Locums Annual Report and had access to the company's books would have identified the following long list of potential causes of its death as a public company:

- Software costs were still capitalised on the balance sheet, even though these assets were no longer being used.
- Accrued revenues were growing fast and becoming a significant component of current assets.
- The costs of employees, as well as external costs incurred in acquiring an internal database of candidates, were capitalised.
- Overpayments by clients (mainly the NHS) were not credited back to them.
- Borrowings were secured on fictitious invoices through an invoice discounting agreement.
- Costs classified as re-organisation costs (and often disregarded by investors) were actually the real costs of running the business.
- Costs were not properly accrued for.

Most of these accounting shenanigans were arguably done to keep profits moving up and to secure borrowings, but unfortunately

An unhealthy share price

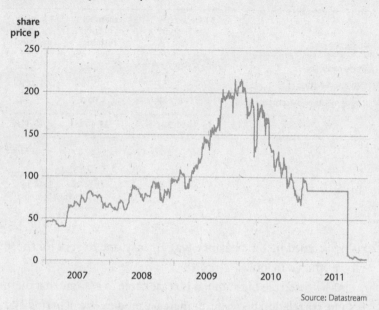

Source: Datastream

for Diane Jarvis, the finance director at the time, the long arm of the Financial Reporting Council finally apprehended her. In 2015 she was banned from the Institute of Chartered Accountants in England and Wales (ICAEW) for ten years and fined £25,000.

First symptoms of disease – rising accrued income

Although there were already symptoms of troubles ahead in 2008, the 2009 Healthcare Locums Annual Report should have put the company firmly in the observation room. It is difficult to identify just one major accounting shenanigan from the plethora of very obvious accounting sleights of hand that were being used, but the

Note 15: Trade and other receivables, an extract, £'000

	31 December 2009	31 December 2008 restated	1 January 2008 restated
Trade receivables	17,594	19,526	20,635
Other receivables	5,053	1,913	2,091
Prepayments and accrued income	8,717	5,970	4,392
	31,364	27,409	27,118

Source: 2009 Healthcare Locums Annual Report

46% increase in accrued income

rising accrued income balance was an easy one to spot for those who bothered to look.

As a broad rule of thumb, it is reasonable to assume that there is some correlation between an increase in sales over a period and the increase in debtors and accrued income. Remember, accrued income is estimated revenue that a company has taken credit for in its income statement which is by its nature a more difficult number to audit than, say, an amount owed by a customer supported by an invoice.

In **Note 15 – Trade and other receivables** (above) in the 2009 Healthcare Locums Annual Report one can see that over the period to end 2009, accrued income had risen by 46% – often symptomatic of aggressive accounting. In contrast, sales over the same period had risen by a paltry 5%. The growth in the accrued income balance therefore had become completely unhinged from the growth in sales. Note 15 also shows a very large increase in other receivables – another warning sign.

Note 14: Other intangible assets, an extract, £'000

	Customer relationships	Computer software	Knowledge database	Candidate database	Total
Cost					
at 1 January 2009	3,953	6,094	100	4,109	14,256
Additions	–	1,572	–	**3,895**	5,467
Disposals	–	(116)	–	–	(116)
at 31 December 2009	3,953	7,550	100	8,004	19,607
Amortisation					
at 1 January 2009	1,038	654	100	1,106	2,898
Provided for the year	439	519	–	2,119	3,077
Disposals	–	(116)	–	–	(116)
at 31 December 2009	1,477	1,057	100	3,225	5,859
Net book value					
at 31 December 2009	2,476	6,493	–	4,779	13,748
at 31 December 2008	2,915	5,440	–	3,003	11,358

Capitalised salaries

Source: 2009 Healthcare Locums Annual Report

Salaries bypass the income statement

Note 14 – Other intangible assets (above) shows that Healthcare Locums was building up costs in its balance sheet for a candidate database, while **Note 1 – Accounting policies** (see next page) clearly states what type of costs were being capitalised: 'direct costs include those of employees as well as external costs incurred in identifying and recruiting the candidates'.

Here it looks like the costs of recruiting the candidates to the database – which were actually Healthcare Locums' own employee costs – were being capitalised. Computer costs look very high, too – this was only a recruitment company, after all!

Note 1: Accounting policies, an extract
Other intangible assets – candidate database

Costs that are directly associated with the production of the candidate database are recognised as intangible assets. Direct costs **include those of employees** as well as external costs incurred identifying and recruiting the candidates. The costs of assembling a candidate database recognised as an asset are amortised as the related candidates accept employment offers. The amortisation is shown as part of Cost of Sales expenses within the Consolidated Statement of Comprehensive Income.

Source: 2009 Healthcare Locums Annual Report

> *Employee costs capitalised*

Note 44: Related party transactions, an extract, £'000

	12 months ended 31 December 2009 Purchased from/ (sold to)	12 months ended 31 December 2008 Purchased from/ (sold to)
Trading transactions		
Charges from MyWorkforce Ltd	24	295
Charges from Nationwide Accreditation Bureau Co Ltd	503	689
Charges to Nationwide Accreditation Bureau Co Ltd	–	(31)
Charges to Montagu Nursing Agencies Ltd	(21)	(303)
Charges to Redwood Group Ltd	(151)	–
Charges to Netengines Holdings Ltd	(17)	–
Total	338	650

MyWorkforceLimited, Nationwide Accreditation Bureau Company Limited, Montagu Nursing Agencies Limited and Redwood Group Limited are related parties to the Company by virtue of a significant shareholder of the Company and close family member of one of the Directors, JS Cariss, owning the majority of the share capital of these companies. Redwood Group Limited is also partly owned by one of the Directors.

Source: 2009 Healthcare Locums Annual Report

And finally

There were related party transactions at Healthcare Locums. The related party to Healthcare Locums was John Cariss, the husband of chief executive Kate Bleasdale, who through six companies was providing and receiving services to and from Healthcare Locums. Details of these related party transactions appeared in **Note 44 – Related party transactions** (opposite) on the penultimate page of the 2009 Healthcare Locums Annual Report. Whilst these transactions were small and clearly disclosed, generally investors should be wary of them as they raise questions of conflict of interest between the company and its directors and their relations.

Lesson

Read an annual report, or indeed an IPO prospectus, by starting from the back. The more interesting stuff tends to be tucked away there. The related party transactions between Healthcare Locums and the chief executive's husband's companies were not the reason that the company went bust, but they were another indicator that things were not quite right.

Erinaceous

COSY CAPITALISM – KEEPING IT IN THE FAMILY

Erinaceous was a one-stop property services company built almost entirely from acquisitions that were not integrated well enough into the group's existing activities, even though the marketing spiel proclaimed 'One Company One Solution'. There was, however, one happy family that controlled the board – which is not usually a good thing.

Neil Bellis, the chief executive, was married to Juliet Bellis (née Cummings). Lucy Cummings, the chief operating officer, was the sister of Juliet Bellis. And they all lived happily together in the same house. Juliet Bellis was a lawyer who every now and then would supply services to Erinaceous. Juliet Bellis was also the company secretary to Erinaceous. Erinaceous sold companies that owned property – to the directors of Erinaceous. Marks out of ten for corporate governance?

There were plenty of related party transactions disclosed in Erinaceous's annual reports. The most significant, in 2002, involved Erinaceous selling a property company to its own directors at seemingly net asset value. A rat should perhaps have been smelled then, as five years later Erinaceous shares were worthless.

Zero to hero to zero

Erinaceous means 'hedgehog-like'. Quite why this was chosen as a name for a fast-growing property services company, perhaps only the old management can tell us. It cannot have occurred to them that the hedgehogs not seen flattened on the road are often riddled with ticks and fleas. One might say that the omens were there early on.

From humble beginnings in 2001, Erinaceous made at least thirty-seven acquisitions during its relatively short life. Each year the acquisitions got bigger. At the time of its demise in April 2008, Erinaceous had twenty principal operating companies all conducting property services of one sort or another.

The trouble was that, whilst chief executive Neil Bellis was busy acquiring companies, chief operating officer Lucy Cummings was not doing much to integrate them, and so they were largely left to their own devices. But who could blame Neil Bellis for going on an acquisition fest? He was buying relatively cheaply and the stock market was re-rating the value of his acquisitions – and also Erinaceous – on the basis of the integration that was (or rather, wasn't) taking place and the synergies that were (or rather, were not) being achieved.

The management at Erinaceous failed to take into account that they were buying asset-light but people-rich businesses and they were taking on a lot of debt to do so. Many of the acquired companies' key people walked once they had sold their business. Other problems surfaced in the form of accusations of malpractice at a couple of the acquired businesses, causing the share price to tank. It was not long before Erinaceous was roadkill.

Share price road killed

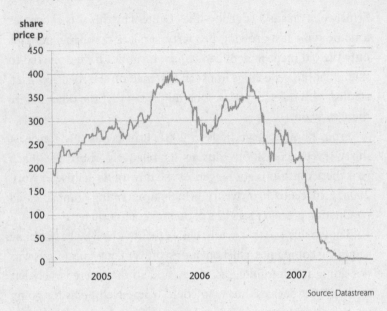

Source: Datastream

Keeping it in the family

Thirty-seven acquisitions in six years is going some, so any investor would need to be certain that the integration of these new companies was going well. This rate of making acquisitions, often for cash and an earn-out, should have been enough to scare sensible investors off.

But the real warning signs that Erinaceous was a risky share were clear as early as 2003, way before the acquisition spree, from the related party transactions note, tucked away, as usual, at the back of the annual report.

To be fair, that much of the legal and secretarial work for Erinaceous was being carried out by the chief executive's wife was

Note 28: Disposals

> *Longmint Limited sold to directors of Erinaceous at close to net asset value*

On 11 April 2002 the Group disposed of its interest in Longmint Limited together with its subsidiaries Proudale Limited and Ground Rental Service Limited. Total consideration for the disposal was **£2,500,000** paid in cash together with the repayment of **£4,500,000** of inter-company debt.

The assets and liabilities disposed of were as follows:

	£000
Intangible fixed assets	(863)
Tangible fixed assets	3,416
Stocks	4,369
Debtors	321
Creditors	(410)
	6,833
	(51)
	6,782
Satisfied by:	
Repayment of inter-company debt	4,282
Cash	2,500
	6,782

Source: 2003 Erinaceous Group Annual Report

disclosed every year in great detail. Not great, but it was no secret and they were not material amounts. On the other hand, however, **Note 28 – Disposals** (above) and **Note 33 – Related party transactions** (see next page) in the 2003 Erinaceous Annual Report disclosed a material transaction that should have put off any investor who chose to look. These notes disclosed that Erinaceous sold a company, whose main assets were stock and property, to its

Note 33: Related party transactions

Juliet Bellis and Co is a related party by virtue of the close family relationship between
J M S Bellis, the principal of Juliet Bellis and Co, and N G Bellis, a director of the company.
Juliet Bellis and Co rendered professional services to the Group amounting to £186,384
(2002: £96,436). The company also received rental income amounting to £5,280 (2002:
£11,400) from Juliet Bellis and Co.

The company disposed of Longmint Limited and its subsidiaries to Longmint Properties
Limited in April 2002. **Longmint Properties Limited is a related party by virtue
of common directors and shareholdings.** The disposal was made at fair value and on
arms-length terms.

Source: 2003 Erinaceous Group Annual Report

> Longmint Properties Limited
> was owned by directors of
> Erinaceous Group

own directors for £7 million. The net assets acquired were valued
at £6.7 million. I have no idea what the realisable value of this
property or stock was, but it is difficult to imagine that the directors
of Erinaceous saw it as a loss-making opportunity for themselves.
And by the way, Note 28 – Disposals shows a negative intangible.
What can that be? This large related party property transaction
should have indicated that the property services company Erinaceous was not as safe as houses, and its directors had too many
potential conflicts of interest.

Lesson

There was plenty going on at Erinaceous to curb one's enthusiasm
to invest in a one-stop property services shop that had been built
largely through acquisitions. On average, Erinaceous was making
six acquisitions a year – which was enough in itself to make one

question whether this was a share worth owning. But, more importantly, it was clear very early on that related party transactions were an issue, especially when the directors sold a company to themselves. Such cosy capitalism is rarely in the interests of ordinary shareholders.

PART 9

Beware of conflict

WHEN AUDITORS GET TOO CLOSE
FOR COMFORT

The Findel share price did not collapse because its auditor undertook significant non-audit services for the company. That is clear. It collapsed for a host of other reasons. But in 2006 the company's auditor – unusual even in those days – received more money for its non-audit work done for Findel than for its audit work. This is an indicator that there may have been a conflict of interest and one of the many warning signs to avoid the shares.

New EU directives will hopefully reduce the risk of conflict involving an auditor, but in the past some auditors have not been too concerned about taking on remunerative non-audit work for companies for which they also carry out the much less rewarding audit work. The 2006 Findel Annual Report demonstrates this. That year its auditors charged £290,000 as an audit fee but £587,000 for non-audit services. The auditors received more for non-audit services than they did for audit services in the previous year as well. It was the same at Enron, although on a much larger scale.

In 2000 Arthur Andersen billed $25 million to Enron for audit services but $27 million for consultancy. Arthur Andersen is no more and the US's Sarbanes–Oxley Act of 2002 has subsequently banned auditors from providing consultancy to its audit clients.

In the past, all that mattered was that the audit committee was happy that the auditor was the most appropriate provider of the non-audit services. Correspondingly, the guidance was that the audit engagement partner – that is, the person who signs off the audit report – should also be happy that the provision of non-audit services by his firm would not compromise his own audit objectivity and independence.

All that has changed for a 'public interest entity' (PIE), that is, a company governed by the law of any EU member state whose transferable securities are traded on a regulated market. The company's audit committee must be happy about the extent of non-audit services provided by the auditor and the auditor must be happy that his independence is not compromised. Non-audit fees must be no more than 70% of the audit fee and certain non-audit services cannot be carried out at all by the auditor. These include tax advice and compliance, services that are involved in managing the entity, book keeping, valuation services, services relating to the financing of the entity, legal services and services related to the shares of the entity. There are of course many who now think that, to ensure no conflicts of interest, non-audit services should not be provided by the auditor.

Findel

'EAR ALL, SEE ALL, SAY NOWT!

Findel was always restructuring itself. Every year, it seemed. Never standing still. And at a cost that was always treated as an exceptional item. Findel even invented a new term, the 'benchmark profit', in order that management's performance could be measured without including these high exceptional costs. Some investors were clearly fooled by this and it was not until the 2007 credit crunch that Findel finally came unstuck – although it is remarkable that it didn't happen way before.

Findel, principally based in Ilkley, West Yorkshire, had two main activities. One was home shopping and the supply of consumer goods on credit (that is, money lending to the less well off); the other was the provision of educational aids, mostly to state schools (which made the business vulnerable to government cuts).

An accounting stretch way too far

The most outrageous accounting practice that Findel engaged in – until 2003 – was the deferral of selling costs. Let's explain. Having borrowed a Findel home shopping catalogue from her next-door neighbour, our fictitious new customer Mrs Barraclough decided to purchase a Russell Hobbs two-slice toaster. At the time, orders from new customers were attracting an introductory discount, but instead of taking this as a cost of sale, as one would expect, Findel accounted for the discount on the toaster as the cost of recruiting Mrs Barraclough and treated it as an asset. This was then written off over the life that Mrs Barraclough was expected to be a customer. The costs to Findel of the catalogue that Mrs Barraclough borrowed from her friend were also capitalised and recorded as an asset in Findel's balance sheet. At its peak, £37 million of these costs were recorded helpfully for Findel as prepayments and accrued income in the balance sheet – a quite staggering amount. In the context of profits, this accounting wheeze arguably overstated profits by nearly 25% in the five years to 2003. This, though, was seemingly not enough to warn off potential investors, as it wasn't until the credit crunch began to bite in 2007 that the company's shares started their collapse. They have never really recovered.

It is not as if the warning signs that the company was heading for a fall had not been there before – the 2006 Findel Annual Report was full of them. Let's begin by listing a few:

- It was an exceptional year that did not include restructuring costs as an exceptional item – and 2006 was no exception. If Findel restructured its activities almost every year, then surely restructuring costs were no longer exceptional.
- So littered were the trading results of the company with significant exceptional costs that Findel decided to introduce and emphasise its own terms, 'benchmark operating profit' and 'benchmark earnings per share' for measuring

Plenty of warning signs

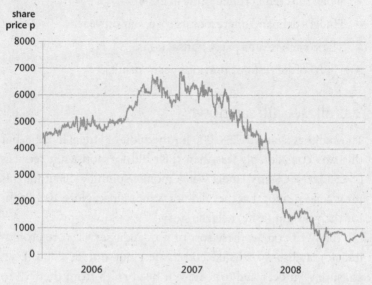

Source: Datastream

management's achievements. These new measures conveniently omitted restructuring costs and painted a much glossier picture of the company's performance.

- By 2006, five of the most senior directors had been with Findel for between nineteen and twenty-five years. It must have been worth it to have been there so long. This length of time for so many to be board directors of a public company is truly exceptional.

- There were very large provisions for doubtful debts, as ladies like Mrs Barraclough sometimes did not pay. In 2006, 24% of the group's receivable was deemed a doubtful debt. Although even this extraordinarily high provision was not high enough when the credit crunch came in 2008.

- Findel's debt and interest costs rose year on year.
- There were related party transactions.
- Findel often restated previous years' results.

'ear all, see all, say nowt!

The auditors charged £290,000 for the audit of Findel in 2006, but this was considerably less than their bill for non-audit services of £587,000. Clearly Findel was a money-spinning client for this provincial auditor that they did not want to lose. **Note 10 – Profit for the year** (opposite) tells the story.

Today, of course, these sort of non-audit services are prohibited for auditors of listed companies, but not in 2006. Even so, surely Findel's auditors did not need rules from the FRC to appreciate that their independence was being compromised. So no rules broken by the auditors then but, according to this illuminating note, the accounts department at Findel needed help with VAT; it needed help about taxes generally; it needed help on corporate finance matters; and it needed help complying with new accounting standards. Which tells you all you need to know about the quality of the accounts department at Findel, and of course that was reflected in the company's annual reports and its ultimate collapse.

Note 10: Profit for the year, an extract

Amounts payable to Deloitte & Touche LLP and their associates by the company and its UK subsidiary undertakings in respect of **non-audit services were £587,000** (2005: £400,000). This principally comprised fees of £122,000 (2005: £149,000) for VAT consultancy, fees of £147,000 (2005: £155,000) for tax related services, fees of £200,000 (2005: £nil) for corporate finance related services and £65,000 (2005: £nil) relating to the group's transition to IFRS.

Included in the above are fees of £7,000 (2005: £7,000) for the audit of the group's pension schemes.

A description of the work of the audit committee is set out in the Audit Committee Report on page 15 and includes an explanation of how auditor objectivity and independence is safeguarded when non-audit services are provided by the auditors.

Source: 2006 Findel Annual Report

> *The fees paid for non-audit services were almost double the £290,000 audit fee for 2006*

Lesson

So much was wrong with Findel that it's a complete mystery as to why banks continued to lend to the company and high-profile investors stayed on board. Because of the Enron disaster, Sarbanes–Oxley and the FRC, auditors are now restricted as to how much tax and related services they can provide to their audit clients, but in 2006 they were less restricted and, by the looks of the note above, Findel's accounts department was well below the standard expected of a publicly listed company. The sheer chutzpah of deferring discounts on sales to new customers in earlier years and calling them customer recruitment costs while recording them as assets was surely enough of a warning sign that Findel was a dangerous share to own.

PART 10

The trend is your friend

FINANCIAL ANALYSIS AND THE USE OF RATIOS

Fund management marketing information that espouses a fund's characteristics and, importantly, its performance often reminds us that 'past performance is not a guide to future performance'. But it can be and, in the case of Toshiba, Interserve and Pets at Home it certainly was.

It is the comparison of financial data often in the form of ratios from one period to another that can highlight a trend – and help one spot both imminent disasters and investment opportunities.

The data and ratios used in financial analysis to gauge a company's performance fall into four categories, enabling one to:

- Monitor activity levels.
- Measure liquidity, or the company's ability to meet short-term cash obligations.
- Assess the company's solvency, or its ability to meet longer-term financial obligations.
- Judge profitability.

Any deterioration in the ratios that monitor these four categories is worthy of investigation and, if it is not in synchrony with a company's share price, that is a forewarning of trouble ahead.

I would add that any financial analysis should also include a thorough review of the changes over time of balance sheet items – for that is often where the bad news is buried. One should especially explore those balances that are most affected by subjective judgements made by management. Net book values of fixed assets are determined by subjective depreciation rates; levels of debtors are determined by subjective bad debt provisions; inventory valuations are very important in determining profits of large manufacturing businesses such as Toshiba and stock obsolescence provisions are subjective; accrued income balances are estimates; and creditors are determined by levels of subjective accruals. In fact, everything is subjective … except cash. There are other things worth looking out for, too. For example, the contributions made from acquisitions tell us a lot about the organic growth rates of companies, as does the analysis of contributions of one-off items such as disposals.

Over the period 2007–2013, Toshiba had sinking sales, a declining depreciation charge, soaring stock levels, reduced cash generation and falling profits, but this painted a much brighter picture than the restated results finally revealed following an enquiry initiated by the Tokyo regulator. This found that profits had been overstated by nearly 40% over the period, but there were worrying signs all along in the financial trends.

One of the tricks of the forensic analyst is to compare one year's numbers in an income statement or balance sheet with the previous year's numbers. In a growing business, which is what you would expect in the case of an IPO, you should see sales and costs increasing in a reasonably linear fashion. This was indeed what was happening at online domestic appliance retailer AO World prior to its flotation in early 2014, apart from one key number in its IPO documentation – its marketing and advertising expenditure. For those who stopped to think about it, it should have been obvious that profits could not be sustained, as marketing and advertising expenditure on the internet and TV was going to rise substantially in the future, just as the AO World prospectus indicated it would.

Interserve went into administration in 2019, yet another support services company disaster in that troubled sector. Interserve appeared to have few financial attractions and it is a mystery why anyone would want to own its equity. A review of its financial track record up to the point the shares were worth nothing revealed that bad debts were significant; there was no cash generation and the company had rising debt; there was little organic growth; and it lived on wafer thin margins where cost overruns would swing Interserve into losses. The margins were just too unsustainably low and long-term survival was unlikely as the line between profits and losses was just too fine.

Pets at Home floated on the London Stock Exchange in 2014. After a reasonable start to life as a public company the shares subsequently tumbled as expectations were not met. But it was obvious from the recent financial record of the company under private equity ownership that the big improvement in profit-ability had already taken place under their ownership, leaving little upside for the enthusiasts who foolishly purchased the shares at flotation. You see, the Pets at Home profitability had already been transformed as dog lovers switched from buying low-margin wet food in tins to higher-margin nutritious dry food in sacks. The clever private equity companies took all the upside leaving the new owners who purchased the shares at float with a bit of a dog's dinner.

AO World

UH OH!

Just £1 – that's what John Roberts won in a bet over a few beers in his local pub when he set up AO World in 2000. But the IPO in 2014 of this online white goods retailer of dishwashers, washing machines and fridges dished up a frothy valuation of £455 million for its founder's shares on the first day of dealing on the London Stock Exchange. He was by all accounts delighted, and who wouldn't be? But any delight for early investors in the company has been short-lived as, having reported decent profits in the year before the flotation, AO World has subsequently tumbled into losses, which show no sign of abating as more advertising expenditure in support of its brand on line and on TV in particular is proving to be a constant drain on profits.

Who could blame John Roberts?

A whopping £1.6 billion – that's what AO World was worth after its first day of trading on the London Stock Exchange. The shares were placed at 285p, making the company worth a modest £1.2 billion, but promptly rose to 378p. They have never hit that level

Tumbling shares

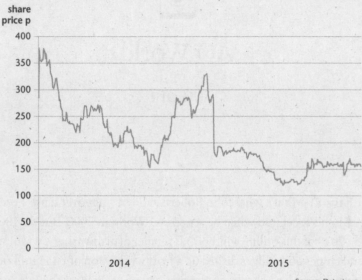

Source: Datastream

again, and towards the end of 2017 were as low as 100p. But who can blame John Roberts for floating the company for £1.2 billion, given that allegedly less than a year before his advisers had told him it was worth just £300 million? Investors who bought shares in the IPO were happy with a price earnings ratio of 180 – the value of the company as a multiple of its after tax earnings – and a market capitalisation to sales ratio of 4.4 – the value of the company as a multiple of its sales. For those who bought at the peak, it appears they were happy to pay a price that represented a stratospheric 240 times historic earnings and 5.8 times sales.

What were investors thinking?

It gets worse – AO World has yet to make a profit since the IPO and the shares have suffered two dramatic price falls, one following flotation in 2014, the other in 2015. What were AO World's new investors thinking when they bought the shares? Perhaps they thought that AO World was going to be the next Amazon – of white goods and appliances. Or that it might be Amazon's next acquisition? Why else would they pay such a high price? But they were missing something that perhaps chairman Richard Rose knew all along as he offloaded 90% of his shares a little more than a year after the IPO. (Rose was replaced in June 2016 by the eminently sensible Geoff Cooper, former chief executive of UK building materials stalwart Travis Perkins.)

If investors at the IPO saw AO World as just another online retailer of white goods and appliances, they were wrong. It was more than that – although not a lot of people knew it. For those who dug a little deeper into the IPO document and annual report, they would have seen that AO World was also in the business of selling product protection plans.

Product protection plans

No one really knows how much AO World makes from selling Domestic & General's product protection plans to its new customers, as it will not tell anyone. But we can have a good stab at it. It appears that the way the sales of the plans are accounted for, this activity currently makes more profits for AO World than selling, delivering and installing washing machines. Arguably, if one were to describe AO World's activities based on where it makes profits rather than where it has the greatest sales, then one

Note 15: Trade and other receivables, £'000

	Year ended 31 March			Nine months ended 31 December	
	2011	2012	2013	2012*	2013
Trade receivables	4,116	2,534	6,457	6,215	7,140
Accrued income (see note 22)	6,520	10,096	14,266	12,962	17,889
Prepayments	4,054	6,008	7,426	6,488	7,349
Amounts due from related parties	–	–	18	–	–
Directors loan account	–	–	57	–	–
	14,690	18,638	28,224	25,665	32,378
The trade and other receivables are classified as:					
Non-current assets	4,890	5,589	9,308	8,690	9,829
Current assets	9,800	13,049	18,916	16,975	22,549
	14,690	18,638	28,224	25,665	32,378

*unaudited
Source: AO World Prospectus

IFRS7 disclosures are included in note 22. Accrued income relates to **expected future commission** payments in respect of product protection plans.

Rising accruals from expected future commissions in respect of product protection plans

could describe it as a sales agent for Domestic & General, whose extended warranty products it sells. But that would make the shares less attractive.

Note 15 – Trade and other receivables (above) from the company prospectus indicates that, as of 31 December 2013, £17.9 million was owed to AO World by Domestic & General in respect of commissions generated from the sales of product protection plans. The £17.9 million represented the estimated fair value of future commissions receivable from Domestic & General over the lives of the product protection plans sold on their behalf by AO World. There is no mention in the note of the fair value being calculated as a result of discounting expected future cash flows, but there is in later annual reports. On the basis that product protection plans last five years on average and that they were sold via a telephone sales operation based at AO World, approximately £3–4 million of profits may have been generated in the year ended March 2014. Of course, cash profits would be completely different. Knowing that a very significant profit stream was generated by the fair value put on future commissions payable by Domestic & General might have discouraged investors from buying shares at 180 times earnings. A more realistic rating of the shares was only a matter of time.

Marketing and advertising

Note 4 – Administrative expenses (see overleaf) from AO World's prospectus indicates that future marketing and advertising expenses were going to rise dramatically, as one can see that for the nine months ended December 2013 they rose from £5.0 million the year before to £12.9 million – that is, a 157% increase.

For the year ended March 2013 and a year before flotation, AO World reported a profit of £8.7 million, with marketing and advertising expenses accounting for just 2.6% of revenues. For the following period marketing and advertising expenses rose to 4.6% of sales, and this trend has continued as AO World spends more and more on supporting its brand on search engines such as Google and on television. As mentioned before, AO World has

Note 4: Administrative expenses comprise the following, an extract, £'000

	Year ended 31 March			Nine months ended 31 December	
	2011	2012	2013	2012*	2013
Marketing and advertising expenses	4,040	6,089	7,131	4,994	12,861
Warehousing expenses	5,162	6,723	9,172	6,314	9,559
Other administrative expenses	15,530	23,337	26,135	17,878	26,577
	24,732	36,149	42,438	29,186	48,997
Marketing and advertising expenses as a % of revenues	2.5	2.9	2.6	2.5	4.6

*unaudited
Source: AO World Prospectus

Dramatic increase in marketing and advertising expenses

not reported a profit since the year before flotation and it could be argued that this is mainly due to its ever-increasing need to spend in support of its own brand. There were perhaps some who missed this important factor as their eyes were drawn to the profit reported in 2013, which was clearly supported by an unsustainably low spend on marketing and advertising.

Lesson

When comparing figures in an annual report for the most recent year against previous years, always try to get an understanding as to why numbers have gone up or down from one period to the other. Bear in mind the levels of activity in the year and how they changed – look at the change in sales to determine this. A very simple rule of thumb is that balance sheet and income statement items should change roughly in line with activity levels, and any number that changes materially more or less than this is worthy of further investigation. The 157% increase in marketing and advertising expenses for the nine months to end December 2013 in AO World's prospectus was just such a number. It was a giveaway that future costs were going to rise and profits were going to fall post IPO.

Toshiba

THE CHALLENGES THAT CREATED TOSH

Some ¥225 billion ($1.9 billion): that's by how much profits at Toshiba had to be reduced following an independent accounting investigation, so that the results for the financial years 2008 to 2014 reflected the reality of its activities over that period rather than what management wanted them to be. In short, Toshiba had overstated its profits by nearly 40% for seven years.

Established in 1904, Toshiba is one of Japan's leading manufacturing companies. Like many Japanese companies it capitalised on the post-war boom in the 1950s and 1960s and expanded its activities into high-growth areas where it manufactured products that met the demands of consumers in the West in particular. It was successful in a wide range of activities that included personal computers, semiconductors, domestic appliances, infrastructure projects and medical equipment. But in 2008, at the onset of the financial crisis, management – firstly under chief executive Atsutoshi Nishida and then under Norio Sasaki and Hisao Tanaka – began to issue 'challenges' to their business unit heads that certain targets be met. The Toshiba culture at the time demanded unquestioning obedience and as often these targets were not even remotely feasible, business unit leaders fearful of losing their jobs resorted to dubious accounting practices to ensure no loss of face and that the 'challenges' were met. It was remarkable, really, that the practice of issuing 'challenges' and the subsequent achievement of those through the use of dodgy accounting could have gone on for so long without being detected by the various internal and external checks and balances employed to monitor such a large company.

What happened at Toshiba was that:

- Between 2008 and 2014, the 'challenges' set from above ensured that profitability on long-term infrastructure projects was overstated.
- There was an under-accrual of expenses.
- Components for the manufacture of PCs were used to 'stuff the channel' (a term used to describe the oversupply of goods into a distribution network to ensure short-term sales targets were met) in a complicated ruse with original equipment manufacturers (OEMs) who were employed to build Toshiba PCs.
- Inventories of semiconductors were nearly always overvalued and not valued at net realisable value.
- Fixed asset depreciation was insufficient and did not reflect the actual use.

Following an announcement in April 2015 that Toshiba had uncovered accounting irregularities, the company's shares fell by over 60%. Not surprisingly, this led to a clean sweep of the board of directors and the initiation of a long-overdue overhaul of the

A challenging ride for investors

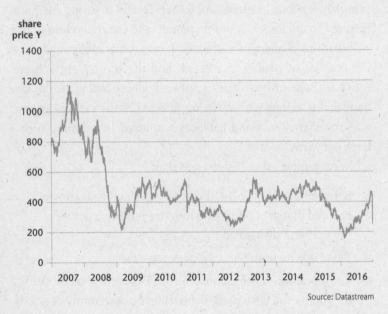

share price Y

Source: Datastream

company culture. But it has been a long haul back and the shares have still to make a full recovery.

Creative and innovative accounting

Toshiba's president and CEO, Hisao Tanaka, was certainly a man true to many of his words when he once said: 'I will do my best to orchestrate Toshiba Group's 200,000 employees' all-out collective efforts to achieve growth through creativity and innovation that will result in higher profitability and will enhance corporate value.'

It is fair to say that he and his predecessors orchestrated the efforts of Toshiba employees by handing down so-called 'challenges' of profit targets to business unit presidents where failure would not be tolerated. This pressure led to creativity and innovation in accounting at the business unit level, which then led to group profits being grossly overstated through a number of techniques. It was a strategy that resulted in the original accounts for 2008 to 2014 being absolute tosh and which certainly did not enhance corporate value. Instead, the shares plummeted.

Unfortunately for Hisao Tanaka and his two predecessors, Norio Sasaki and Atsutoshi Nishida, the Securities and Exchange Surveillance Commission in Tokyo got a whiff that all was not right at Toshiba and made contact with the company in February 2015. The commission required further information on long-term contracts, where the percentage of completion accounting method had been employed. What at first was an internal Toshiba enquiry into long-term contract accounting, prompted by enquiries from the Tokyo regulator, quickly mushroomed into a more general independent investigation into other accounting matters. The amount of overstatement of profits from 2008 to 2014 was eventually calculated at ¥225 billion, or US$1.9 billion. There were four main areas where the so-called 'challenges' issued by senior management had caused their subordinates to initiate inappropriate accounting transactions in order to ensure that targets were met and they kept their jobs. These included:

■ Percentage of completion accounting – in large infrastructure contracts, estimated total cost to completion was not calculated based on the latest information of actual costs incurred, so that provisions for losses were not made. Estimates of total costs to completion were often calculated in anticipation of unsubstantiated cost reductions. The negative adjustment that had to be made to 2008–2014 reported profits in respect of the accounting for these large infrastructure projects was ¥48 billion.

- PC business – Toshiba outsourced the manufacture of its PCs. By supplying components to the outsourcers at an inflated price and also by supplying more components than they required, profits were overstated by ¥58 billion between 2008 and 2014. In addition, the accruals method of recognising expenses was not employed in the PC business and inappropriate profits were booked between group companies.

- Semiconductor inventories – these were not valued, as they should have been, at either cost or net realisable value, whichever was lower. This is curious, as the price of semiconductors can be volatile but in general it fell between 2008 and 2014. Losses on these inventories were only realised once they were sold. Inventory valuation therefore was overstated and, as any accountant knows, closing stock values are key to determining profits. By deferring the downward revaluation of inventory on an ongoing basis Toshiba deferred the reporting of losses on them. As a result, profits were overstated by ¥37 billion between 2008 and 2014.

- Fixed assets – depreciation at many of Toshiba's business units failed to keep up with the use of these assets over time. This happened at the TV, PC and semiconductor business units. A depreciation adjustment was made so that profits over the 2008–2014 period were reduced by ¥47 billion.

A summary of all the required adjustments is shown overleaf in an extract from the 2015 Toshiba Annual Report.

Income (loss) before income taxes, ¥ billion

Restatement of past financial results and effects of restatement

	2008	2009	2010	2011	2012	2013	2014 (1-3 Q cumulative)	Cumulative (2008-14 3Q)
(Before correction)								
Income (loss) before income taxes	-259.7	27.2	194.7	145.4	159.6	180.9	134.9	583.0
Percentage-of-completion method	-3.6	0.1	7.0	-7.9	-18.0	-24.5	-1.0	-47.9
Recording of operating expenses etc in the visual products business	-5.3	-7.8	-6.5	12.7	-2.8	0.8	2.8	-6.1
Component transactions etc in the PC business	-19.8	-28.6	11.3	-22.3	-28.1	10.4	19.3	-57.8
Valuation of inventory etc in the semiconductor business	0.0	-4.4	-1.6	-10.3	-36.6	16.3	-0.5	-37.1
Self-check etc	-6.0	-3.8	-3.4	-7.3	-12.9	-12.2	16.2	-29.4
Amount for impairment of fixed assets	-41.7	3.0	0.3	-48.9	13.7	10.6	16.5	-46.5
Total amount of correction	-76.4	-41.5	7.1	-84.0	-84.7	1.4	53.3	-224.8
(After correction)								
Income (loss) before income taxes	-336.1	-14.3	201.8	61.4	74.9	182.3	188.2	358.2

Source: 2015 Toshiba Annual Report

TOSHIBA

Consolidated financial summary, an extract, ¥ billion

Year ended March 31	2007	2008	2009	2010	2011	2012	2013	
Net sales	6,859.7	7,404.3	6,512.7	6,291.2	6,398.5	6,100.3	5,800.3	*Declining sales*
Cost of sales	5,115.3	5,548.7	5,242.5	4,852.0	4,897.5	4,635.2	4,384.4	
Selling, general and administrative expenses	1,497.2	1,615.2	1,503.6	1,314.0	1,260.7	1,262.4	1,221.6	
Operating income (loss)	247.2	240.4	(233.4)	125.2	240.3	202.7	194.3	
Income (loss) from continuing operations, before income taxes and noncontrolling interests	315.9	258.1	(261.5)	34.4	195.5	145.6	155.6	*No profit growth*
Income taxes	152.5	110.5	61.6	33.5	40.7	64.2	59.9	
Net income (loss) attributable to shareholders of Toshiba Corporation	137.4	127.4	(343.6)	(19.7)	137.8	70.1	77.5	
EBITDA	639.2	676.0	119.6	367.1	486.6	427.0	406.0	
Operating income ratio (%)	3.6	3.2	(3.6)	2.0	3.8	3.3	3.4	
Return on sales (%)	2.0	1.7	(5.3)	(0.3)	2.2	1.1	1.3	
Cost of sales ratio (%)	74.6	74.9	80.5	77.1	76.5	76.0	75.6	
Selling, general and administrative expenses ratio (%)	21.8	21.8	23.1	20.9	19.7	20.7	21.1	
Total assets	5,932.0	5,935.6	5,453.2	5,451.2	5,379.3	5,752.7	6,106.7	
Equity attributable to shareholders of Toshiba Corporation	1,108.3	1,022.3	447.3	797.4	868.1	863.5	1,034.5	
Interest-bearing debt	1,158.5	1,261.0	1,810.7	1,218.3	1,081.3	1,235.8	1,471.6	
Long-term debt	956.2	740.7	776.8	960.9	769.5	909.7	1,038.5	*Rising debt*
Short-term debt	202.3	520.3	1,033.9	257.4	311.8	326.1	433.1	
Shareholders' equity ratio (%)	18.7	17.2	8.2	14.6	16.1	15.0	16.9	
Debt/equity ratio (times)	1.0	1.2	4.0	1.5	1.2	1.4	1.4	

Source: 2012 Toshiba Annual Report

continued >

Consolidated financial summary, an extract, ¥ billion, continued

Year ended March 31	2007	2008	2009	2010	2011	2012	2013	
R&D expenditures	365.3	370.3	357.5	311.8	319.7	319.9	305.9	
Capital expenditures (property, plant and equipment)	373.8	464.5	355.5	209.4	231.0	299.1	237.3	
Depreciation (property, plant and equipment)	258.8	339.4	306.9	252.5	215.7	203.3	171.3	*Falling depreciation*
Return on investment (ROI) (%)	10.6	9.2	(8.9)	5.1	10.4	8.6	7.3	
Return on equity (ROE) (%)	13.0	12.0	(46.8)	(3.2)	16.6	8.1	8.2	
Return on total assets (ROA) (%)	2.6	2.1	(6.0)	(0.4)	2.5	1.3	1.3	
Inventory turnover (times)	9.36	8.96	8.09	8.10	7.71	6.98	6.15	*Rising inventory days*
Total assets turnover (times)	1.29	1.25	1.14	1.15	1.18	1.10	0.98	
Inventory turnover (days)	39.01	40.74	45.11	45.08	47.35	52.31	59.38	
Net cash provided by (used in) operating activities	561.5	247.1	(16.0)	451.4	374.1	335.0	132.3	*Falling cash generation*
Net cash used in investing activities	(712.8)	(322.7)	(335.3)	(252.9)	(214.7)	(377.2)	(196.3)	
Net cash provided by (used in) financing activities	154.8	46.6	478.5	(277.9)	(154.7)	(0.2)	41.8	
Effect of exchange rate changes on cash and cash equivalents	34.9	(31.7)	(32.0)	3.0	(13.3)	(2.1)	17.1	
Net increase (decrease) in cash and cash equivalents	38.4	(60.7)	95.2	(76.4)	(8.6)	(44.5)	(5.1)	
Cash and cash equivalents at end of year	309.3	248.6	343.8	267.4	258.8	214.3	209.2	
Debt/cash flow ratio (%)	41.46	41.96	0.40	18.44	34.57	27.60	21.81	
Interest coverage ratio (times)	8.5	6.7	(6.4)	3.7	7.7	6.7	6.3	
Free cash flow	(151.3)	(75.6)	(351.3)	198.5	159.4	(42.2)	(64.0)	*326 billion yen consumed in 2007–2013*
Market capitalization	2,533.4	2,155.9	822.4	2,046.8	1,724.7	1,542.5	2,000.1	

Source: 2012 Toshiba Annual Report

The trend is your friend

In an analysis of a company's accounts, as the old investment rule goes, a trend can be your friend. So it could have been for anyone who chose to look at Toshiba's accounts. In the 2012 Toshiba Annual Report for the year ended 31 March 2013 (published before the large accounting adjustments were made), there is a very helpful Consolidated Financial Summary of the performance of the group from 2003 to 2013. Our analysis will focus on the latter period from 2007 to 2013 (see the **Consolidated Financial Summary** on pages 240–1). Apart from there being no growth in sales or profit over the period (which are good reasons alone not to own or buy shares), there were some other trends that were quite disturbing and which could have provided a clue to the large accounting adjustments that were to come at Toshiba.

- In a set of accounts, the values attributed to sales, profits, what others owe you (receivables) and what you owe others (payables) are subjective. Cash, on the other hand, is difficult to manipulate and so an analysis of it is important in seeing how well a company is doing. Ideally a company should be cash-generative and, if it is not, there will be trouble ahead eventually. Toshiba was most definitely not a cash-generative company according to the Consolidated Financial Summary in its 2012 Annual Report. From 2006 to 2012 Toshiba consumed ¥326 billion (US$2.8 billion).

- Depreciation is the systematic allocation of the cost of an asset over its estimated useful life. It is accounted for as a cost in the income statement and therefore as a reduction in profits. It can be a material item in the income statement and therefore a main determinant as to the size of profits that are reported by a company, in particular a manufacturing company like Toshiba. Depreciation fell sharply as a charge in Toshiba's accounts between 2006 and 2012 and also fell as a percentage of total assets. A sign perhaps that depreciation was understated?

■ In an ideal world, for a company like Toshiba inventory needs to turn over quickly so that it is not caught out with old or obsolete stock of semiconductors, personal computers and TVs. From 2006 to 2012 the inventory turnover period rose 51% from 39 days to 59 days, a possible indication that Toshiba was holding increasingly obsolete stock – which indeed turned out to be the case.

Lesson

Toshiba is a complicated company. It does a lot of different things. Looking at a set of accounts in isolation for a company like this can be confusing and difficult to analyse. It is much easier to look at the accounts, compare them with others from previous years over time and then search out trends.

Toshiba helpfully provided a simple summary of trends, which it called a Consolidated Financial Summary, at the back of its 2012 annual report. The patterns and changes in numbers revealed that key performance indicators were deteriorating. In simple terms, changes in balance sheet items that are unexplained by activity levels (in other words, a change in the level of sales) need investigating. For example, according to the summary in the 2012 Toshiba Annual Report, inventory levels rose 30% from 2006 to 2012 but sales fell materially over that period. Curiously, Toshiba continually consumed cash even though it reported profits and the depreciation charge fell even though total assets rose in the period. Balance sheet and income statement items should move more or less in some correlated way from year to year. They did not at Toshiba, indicating that the accounts were tosh.

Interserve

A RUBBISH JOB

It was rubbish that finally did for Interserve. It failed to manage the technology and partner risk as its ill-advised diversification into a series of waste-to-energy contracts resulted in large losses that it was unable to finance. In 2019, Interserve collapsed into administration as its shareholders and lenders failed to agree on a way of refinancing yet another problematical outsourcing company. But Interserve had been wasting away for some time, with its share price whittled down year after year. The company was worth over £1 billion in the early part of 2014 but by the time its lenders took control in 2019 it was worth nothing.

Interserve was a Carillion doppelgänger just as Carillion was an Amey doppelgänger. In the world of public sector work and outsourcing where clients are slow payers and always grumble about costs, and where margins can be thin, especially in construction contracts, it is difficult to make ends meet especially where there are cost over-runs on large projects. This was the case at both Carillion and Amey as well as at Interserve. Auditors and management have often failed to quantify the risks in these types of businesses where outcomes on contracts can be wildly over optimistic.

Like Carillion and to an extent Amey before it, Interserve was a mixture of low-margin construction and outsourcing businesses with poor cash flow characteristics because they were often dependent on government and large organisations paying up but which did so slowly. Profits were squeezed further by a rising minimum wage and tightly priced construction contracts where there was often no margin for error. But as late as 2018, just a year before it collapsed, Interserve claimed it was 'one of the world's foremost support services, construction and equipment companies ... offering advice, design, construction, equipment facilities management and frontline services to clients in more than 40 countries'. It had a workforce of 68,000 and revenues of £2.9 billion. For a company that kept on reporting losses or meagre profits at best, one could easily accuse Interserve of being hyperactively foolish. It was a muddled jumble of disparate businesses that lacked focus. At one end of the activity spectrum, it cleaned the platforms at St Pancras station in London; at the other end it was building a proton beam therapy centre for the NHS (its first high-energy cancer treatment centre) that contained 48,000 tons of concrete – twice the weight of an aircraft carrier, Interserve proclaimed.

These activities were a far cry from its 1884 origins when two brothers formed the London and Tilbury Lighterage Company, which transferred cargo between ships in the Thames. The company added dredging activities at the beginning of the twentieth century and then moved into waste and civil engineering in the 1930s–1950s. Construction activities followed and it deployed into the Middle East. In 2001, the firm was renamed

Interserve and under a new management team it acquired Rent-okil's Initial Facilities business for £250 million. Debt started to rise to a worrying level. Interserve was never a very cash genera-tive business but it was its move into rubbish that really started to consume cash and incur losses. It may have been able to handle the construction risk but it had little expertise in turning waste into energy and the process risks involved.

Rubbish contracts

Losses on two waste-to-energy contracts in Glasgow and Derby in particular caused a lot of the damage. In all, the loss on Interserve's waste-to-energy contracts was at least £250 million. This was very unhelpful for debt levels. In 2012 there was virtually no debt on the balance sheet. By the end of 2018 there was £630 million of debt and the management team that had been responsible for incurring it had been replaced. Interserve's debt started changing hands and hedge funds now owned it alongside the banks. A refinancing of over £200 million in 2017 by hedge funds increased their power over the company and they ended up in the driving seat. The casualties were the shareholders, who got nothing when the company went into administration in March 2019 and its assets were transferred to a company controlled by Interserve's lenders. Among the casualties, to the surprise of many, was Coltrane Asset Management, a US hedge fund that had previously made millions from betting that the share prices of Carillion and Mitie, two other support services companies with characteristics similar to Interserve, would fall. Funny that they did not spot that Interserve would do just the same.

A wasting share price

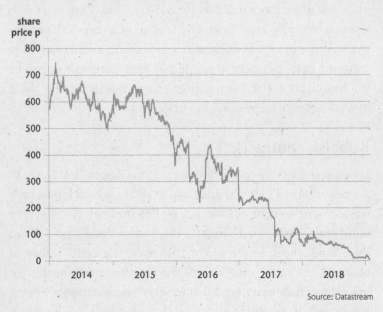

Source: Datastream

Wasting away

Once Interserve's 2014 results were published, the shares began their gentle glide to zero. There was turbulence in the share price when Interserve announced that its waste-to-energy contracts were not going well at all and large losses were going to be reported on them. However, even though the distress signs were there in the annual reports that followed, it was a five-year glide before the share price finally hit the ground.

The usual deterioration in current asset quality and related rise in accrued income associated with other similar disastrous support service companies may not have been present but there

were just as obvious signs in the annual reports that Interserve was going to be a poor investment:

■ Interserve was an exceptional company in that it just about always reported exceptional items in its income statement. Any company that regularly records costs as exceptional items is to be avoided. In Interserve's case, there were not only the costs relating to the losses incurred on the waste-to-energy contracts but other large exceptional losses on asset impairments, contract reviews and advisers' fees. Between 2013 and 2018 these exceptional amounts accounted for a massive £746 million of losses.

■ Cash as they say is king, but there was nothing regal about cash at Interserve because from 2013 onwards there was none. Only debt that rose every year. Losses on the waste-to-energy contracts, capital expenditure, extra pension contributions and losses on its joint ventures all took their toll. A company that has rising debt and little forward movement in profits is a company that slowly transfers its value from its equity holders to its debt holders, which is of course exactly what happened with Interserve.

■ Bad debts took their toll too. From 2012 to 2018 support services and equipment sales appeared to suffer bad debts of between 10% and 14% of amounts invoiced. These activities made up two-thirds of Interserve's sales and indicated that this business was low quality. But then so were the construction activities, with much of the business in the Middle East and Africa, where arguably there was more uncertainty, with margins varying from less than 1% to 3.4% between 2014 to 2018. And that was all before the

Significant bad debts

Little organic growth excluding 2014 where growth was largely due to acquisitions

Interserve analysis, an extract, £m

Trade and other receivables	2018	2017	2016	2015	2014	2013	2012
Trade debtors	354.2	384.4	380.7	444.5	418.0	290.8	270.1
Bad debts	**−38.5**	**−47.5**	**−54.3**	**−46.3**	**−49.2**	**−41.8**	**−30.5**
	315.7	336.9	326.4	398.2	368.8	249.0	239.6
Bad debts %	**10.9**	**12.4**	**14.3**	**10.4**	**11.8**	**14.4**	**11.3**
Sales	2904.0	3250.8	3244.6	3204.6	2913.0	2192.6	1958.4
Sales growth %	**−10.7**	**0.2**	**1.2**	**10.0**	**32.9**	**12.0**	**6.0**
PBT before exceptional items	13.7	52.4	137.3	115.4	106.2	81.1	75.3
Exceptional items	**−125.0**	**−296.8**	**−231.4**	**−35.9**	**−44.3**	**−13.0**	**104.5**
PBT	−111.3	−244.4	−94.1	79.5	61.9	68.1	179.8
Margin %	0.5	1.6	4.2	3.6	3.6	3.7	3.8
Borrowings							
Cash	196.7	155.1	113.3	86.1	82.1	79.7	76.8
Bank overdraft	0.0	−6.8	−11.1	−15.5	5.5	−27.4	−19.8
Bank loans	−827.5	−647.5	−449.4	−406.1	−362.8	−90.0	−30.0
Total debt	**630.8**	**499.2**	**347.2**	**335.5**	**275.2**	**37.7**	**27.0**
Cash consumed	**131.6**	**152.0**	**11.7**	**60.3**	**237.5**	**64.7**	**−70.2**

Source: 2012–2018 Interserve Annual Reports

Almost always costly exceptional items

Rising debt

No cash generation – 2012 cash distorted by disposal proceeds

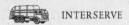

contract reviews and asset impairments mentioned above.

- When things were not going well at Interserve, there was an emphasis on reporting so-called 'headline profit before tax' and 'headline earnings per share' in order to present a rosier picture of trading by omitting all the large important exceptional costs.

In summary, the Interserve annual reports told us that the company's activities were low quality because they were low margin and cash generation was poor. There was a lot of execution risk on top of this which got even worse as the waste-to-energy contracts started. There was no margin for error. It was a rubbish business that even new management in the form of the formidable Debbie White from Sodexo found impossible to rescue. If there was ever one company where the signs really were there in abundance, it was Interserve.

Hyperactively foolish

Interserve was a very low-margin business. It reported 2% to 3% operating margins after exceptional items between 2013 and 2015 before it lurched into the continuous losses from which it never recovered. Low-margin businesses are fine as long as there is growth, quick cash collection and no surprises. But Interserve did not really grow organically, cash generation was poor and there were many surprises. It was obvious that there was no margin for error, in particular as the company started building waste-to-energy plants for local authorities that failed to turn out as planned and where the completion risk for the projects largely remained with Interserve.

Pretty much the biggest number in the 2014 Interserve

Note 19: Construction Contracts, an extract, £m
Balances relate to contracts in progress at the balance sheet date

	Dec 2014	Dec 2013	Dec 2012
Contract costs incurred plus recognised profits and losses	4886.1	4938.6	4698.0
less progress billings	-4838.6	-4915.6	-4667.7
	47.5	23.0	30.3

Source: Interserve 2014 Annual Report

High value construction contracts with no margin for error

Annual Report was £4.9 billion. This represented the construction costs incurred plus recognised profits less recognised losses to date for contracts in progress up to the end of 2014 – see **Note 19 Construction Contracts** (above). This emphasised just how susceptible profits at Interserve were to small changes in this large number. Put it this way: a 1% error in estimating or recording these construction costs or estimating or recording profits or losses on the contracts pretty much wiped out annual profits at Interserve because its margins were so small.

This was enough of a warning sign and when Interserve entered into waste-to-energy contracts under which it was responsible for building and operating the facilities for a fixed price the whole business got even riskier.

Lesson

Low-margin businesses that fail to generate cash are a disaster waiting to happen. It's only a matter of time before a large contract

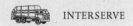

goes wrong and losses are reported. Lenders then say enough is enough and will not provide any more cash. Analysis of the 2014 Interserve Annual Report published years before Interserve's demise told us that this was a poor company that was fighting hard just to stay afloat. You can only fight hard for a limited time on low margins and no positive cash flow before the unexpected happens, contracts go wrong, losses are reported and the share price falls.

Pets at Home

FOR LAP DOGS

Attitudes to pets in the UK have changed. We have humanised them and now treat them like people. That means we groom them; we put coats on them in the winter; we feed them better than we did; we want our pooches to have a healthy coat and teeth and so we nourish them well with more expensive and nutritious food. We also want to make it easier to scoop their poop and by feeding them with dry food there is less likely to be a terrible mishap. A pet is now quite likely to visit a vet more times than its owner goes to the doctor. The founder of Pets at Home, Anthony Preston, realised all this and from opening his first store in 1991, he built up a chain of pet stores, many of which offered grooming and veterinary services. Importantly, he also launched a dry pet food branded Wainwrights.

At the time of its flotation in 2014, Pets at Home was a clear market leader with about 370 stores – nearly 150 more than its five nearest competitors had in total. Its size gave it considerable purchasing power, especially when sourcing from Asian producers, which in turn gave it a significant competitive edge when it came to pricing.

The company had been cleverly acquired by private equity firm Bridgepoint in 2004 and then sold on in 2010 to KKR, another private equity firm. After a short period of ownership KKR decided to list the shares of Pets at Home on the London Stock Exchange (LSE) and the glossy IPO prospectus published in early 2014 highlighted a performance track record that showed that both sales and adjusted profits for the five years to 2013 had grown by 11% every year – see **Non-IFRS measures of performance 2008–13** (below). Investors were impressed and snapped up the shares. But there were some who thought that it was all too good to be sustained, pointing to signs that activity levels demonstrated in changes in the like-for-like sales, were on the wane and margins had peaked.

Non-IFRS measures of performance 2008–13, an extract, £m

	FY08	FY09	FY10	FY11	FY12	FY13
Revenue	354.6	404.3	467.7	508.2	544.3	598.3
Adjusted EBITDA	60.7	70.0	84.3	92.3	94.1	102.1
Adjusted EBITDA margin	17.1%	17.3%	18.0%	18.2%	17.3%	17.1%
Unlevered free cashflow	45.8	54.9	67.3	73.0	76.3	88.7
Like-for-like sales growth	8.0%	7.5%	8.8%	1.6%	1.3%	2.4%
Store numbers	213	232	256	281	313	345

Source: 2014 Pets at Home Prospectus

11% compound sales and EBITDA growth

Flat margins

Slowing like-for-like sales growth

A dog of a share price

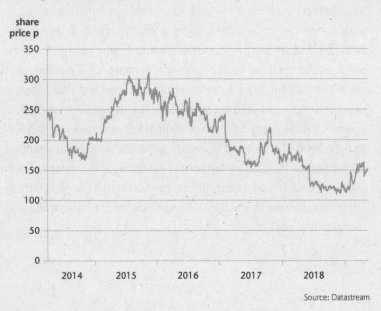

Source: Datastream

Promising pup of a company

Pets at Home had a muted start to life as a public company but its shares eventually went to a healthy premium in the period after it floated on the LSE. But in late 2015, everything started to go downhill. Like-for-like sales growth slowed further, the rise in the National Living Wage and more expensive imports, as a result of a weakening in sterling all cut into margins. Earnings per share growth was non-existent and there were too many changes in management. It was a dog's dinner and shareholders were the ones left in the dog house as the share price collapsed some 60% in three years. By mid-2019, however, a new management team was achieving impressive like-for-like sales growth again which had a positive impact on the share price due to selling more pet services.

Top dog food

Pets at Home's success, as Matt Davies who had been appointed CEO in 2004, explained to me late on a Friday in 2010 prior to the sale to KKR, was down to persuading the great British dog-owning public to move from buying wet dog food in tins to dry advanced nutrition food in bags and cartons. This transformed margins at Pets at Home – see the **Adjusted profit and loss account 2003–2010** (overleaf). Dog food accounts for about 40% of Pets at Home's sales and between 2003 and 2010 the substantial shift to dry food (on which the margin is 40% to 60% versus 9% to 12% for wet food) is the main reason that the gross margin at Pets at Home moved from 38% to 52% and its operating margin tripled from 5% to 15% in the period 2003 to 2010. The effect of this transition, and indeed the increased direct sourcing from the Far East that avoided the need for agents, may have accounted for the vast majority of the increased profit in the period. Like a young dog that has learned a new trick and is eager to learn another, Pets at Home needed a new trick to keep the dog show on the road. But what?

KKR clearly thought that new tricks were in the offing as they acquired Pets at Home for £955 million in 2010, which by all accounts was around eight times what Bridgepoint had paid for the company six year earlier. Reported sales and profits continued to grow in the short term despite the unexpected departure in 2011 of Matt Davies, and when it floated in 2014 the value of Pets at Home was £1.2 billion – a nutritious return for KKR after just a

Adjusted profit and loss accounts 2003–2010, an extract, £'000

Year ended 31st March	As reported 2010	As reported 2009	Adjusted 2008	Adjusted 2007	Adjusted 2006	Adjusted 2005	Adjusted 2004	Adjusted 2003
Sales	462,646	399,899	350,800	303,152	272,233	253,701	213,714	201,625
Cost of goods sold	222,891	195,706	282,609	251,955	230,938	219,050	191,217	181,225
Adjustment	–	–	(87,710)	(78,196)	(71,674)	(67,984)	(59,346)	(56,245)
Adjusted cost of sales	222,891	195,706	194,899	173,759	159,264	151,066	131,871	124,980
Gross profit	239,755	204,193	155,901	129,393	112,969	102,635	81,843	76,645
Gross profit %	52	51	44	43	41	40	38	38
Operating costs	172,110	146,004	15,282	12,508	15,542	11,916	9,789	9,899
Adjustment	–	–	87,710	78,196	71,674	67,984	59,346	56,245
Adjusted operating costs	172,110	146,004	102,992	90,704	87,216	79,900	69,135	66,144
Operating profit	67,645	58,189	52,909	38,689	25,753	22,735	12,708	10,501
Operating profit %	15	15	15	13	9	9	6	5

Source: 2003–2010 Pets at Home Annual Reports

Significant rise in operating profit margin as a result of gross margins on dog food falling through to bottom line. In 2009 the operating profit margin improvement clearly ceased.

Significant rise in gross profit margin as a result of consumers' preference for dry food over wet food for dogs. In 2010 the gross profit margin improvement clearly ceased.

few years of ownership. Since then investors in Pets at Home over the long term have not done so well. But for anyone who read the IPO prospectus with care, it was clear that the future was unlikely to be quite as bright as the past as both private equity companies, Bridgepoint and KKR, had reaped the benefits from the earlier fundamental changes in the eating habits of man's best friend.

The table opposite shows an adjusted profit and loss account extracted from Pets at Home annual reports for the period up to 2010. It is adjusted to ensure that certain costs that in the past were recorded in cost of sales are recorded in operating costs so that periods are comparable and we can see the trend in the improvement in both gross and operating margins. The table clearly shows that operating margins and gross margins had peaked well before the IPO of Pets at Home.

Lesson

There is often only one reason that a private equity firm sells out of an investment. It has done all it can to maximise profits and now wishes to sell the company to others as the future may well not be as bright as the past. In the case of Pets at Home there had been a major change over the period up to the flotation in what dogs were eating and the company had taken full advantage of this. All this meant that profits were transformed as many customers switched from buying wet food in tins to dry food in packets. But anyone could have spotted this change by glancing through the historic annual reports. A gross margin improvement of 38% to 52% over a seven-year period for a retailer is not common, especially these days, and potential investors would have been wise to think that it was not likely to get better than that. The improvement in gross margins fed down to a rise in operating profit margins from 5% to 15% in 2010. The reason that Pets at Home was attractive to the clever private equity investors at Bridgepoint was that they could see this important change was taking place. Once it had happened they were out. Which makes one wonder what the new lapdog investors, who took the shares when Pets at Home floated, thought was going to drive the company forward in the future. The transformational event had come and gone and Bridgepoint and KKR had taken the money and run. Luckily for the current investors at Pets at Home, new management are successfully initiating a strategy that is capturing a greater share of the customer's pet care spend that includes services and products.

PART 11

Never be too starry-eyed

THE DANGER WHEN FUND MANAGERS U-TURN

This book is mostly about companies that collapsed but where just a browse through the annual report would have indicated that the shares were heading for a fall. In nearly all cases, the annual report told us that past profits were overstated and in the future, it would be difficult for the company to keep the show on the road. But many people invest not directly in companies but in investment funds, which are run by people whose job it is to pour through the constituents of their fund and determine whether they are appropriate to meet the objectives of the clients the fund is targeted at, as well as taking other crucial matters into consideration.

Neil Woodford, at Invesco Perpetual, and Anthony Bolton, at Fidelity, before him, were the UK's first star fund managers and rightly so. Both of these money men ran funds that produced exceptional performance against their respective peer groups over a long period of time. Neil Woodford had made investors more than twenty times their money over the twenty-five years he was with Invesco Perpetual, skilfully steering his gigantic income funds through the stormy waters of the tech bubble in 2000 and the financial crisis in 2008.

But instead of quitting while at the top, these two stars decided that they could replicate their success in a new investment game. As it turned out they could not and they became croppers by not sticking to what they knew best and what they had proved themselves good at. Anthony Bolton started a China fund, investing in a market he had little experience in or knowledge of, and its performance was dismal. Neil Woodford started a fund that invested in smaller and unquoted companies, and within a few years found himself having to take the reputation destroying step of suspending dealings in the heavily promoted and popular Woodford Equity Income Fund (WEIF)

The WEIF is an example of where, even though many of the individual holdings were inappropriate for the prevailing economic conditions at that time in that there was over reliance on the UK's domestic economy holding up, the more serious problem was that there were acute structural flaws in the fund's composition and the strategy that it adopted. These flaws revealed themselves when in June 2019 the fund was suspended, locking investors out of £3.6 billion of their money.

The WEIF investment strategy was entirely different to the one Woodford had pursued at Invesco Perpetual. He did a U-turn and rotated his tried and tested investment strategy on its head. Instead of investing all the savings of his adoring investors in high dividend paying large so-called blue-chip companies, he chose to invest in a large number of smaller and unquoted companies that were often the absolute opposite of high dividend paying as many of them actually required cash to survive and grow. There was also a complete disregard to maintain the liquidity of the large WEIF so that investors were able to realise their investments if they wished to cash in.

All this was obvious from the helpful WEIF monthly fund fact sheets readily available to anyone who wished to read them. It was also obvious to many who saw Woodford Investment Management as a competitor and his new investment style was often the talk of the City. It is a mystery to many as to why those who are paid to know these things failed to spot what was so obvious to many others. The debacle has yet to fully play out, but there will be implications that may well hinder the active fund management industry to go about its business as it has done in the past, and the ability of UK smaller companies generally to raise funds on our financial markets – a thing that hitherto we have been rather good at.

Woodford Equity Income Fund

HUBRIS TO HUMBLE PIE

Neil Woodford was known by some as 'The Oracle of Oxford'. He was a hero with no other fund manager bearing comparison in his specialist field – the management of income funds. His performance at Invesco Perpetual was stellar where he made lucky investors 23 times their money for those that backed him when he started running money to when he departed to set up Woodford Investment Management (WIM), just up the A4074 from his old shop.

At his peak, the somewhat remote Neil Woodford ran a staggering £25 billion for UK investors when he was firmly ensconced at Invesco Perpetual. His success was due to getting big calls right. Not big calls picking the right company as he ran so much money that making overweight investments in one or two companies was never going to make a difference. Crucially, he got his sector calls right. In the tech boom leading up to 2000, he steered clear of IT companies with racy accounting and high valuations and benefited as these stocks subsequently collapsed because he had none of them. In the same way he cunningly avoided financials in the run up to the 2008 banking crisis. He stuck to investing the bulk of his funds in boring and unfashionable sectors including tobacco, utilities and pharmaceuticals which importantly had the required cash flow to pay dividends that ultimately provided the cash for him to satisfy his income hungry investors, many of whom were retired. He was to forget this important mantra later when he set out on his own, but it was on these clever calls that Neil Woodford made his mark as he avoided the worst of the market falls. By not following the crowd, he became mainstream investors' favourite UK fund manager.

In 2014, after some lean years of below par performance, Neil Woodford left Invesco Perpetual and with Craig Newman, a former colleague, he set up WIM. There were no independent directors, which was curious for a company that took in so much of the public's money and which was regulated by the FCA – an organisation whose aim is 'to make financial markets work well so that consumers get a fair deal'. Woodford and Newman were joint owners of the new firm and were to benefit considerably from the payment of a dividend of £36.5 million for 2017–18. Staff at WIM, on the other hand, were not so lucky and did not get paid bonuses on the grounds that 'bonuses can lead to short-term decision making' and 'don't work as a motivator'. WIM preferred to pay enhanced salaries to staff, depriving them of the skin in the game that the two founders clearly had. Some would say that this was not a great motivational strategy.

WIM got off to a cracking start and raised £1.6 billion for the Woodford Equity Income Fund (WEIF) soon after launch in July 2014 – a UK record. In 2015, the WEIF produced a return of 16% easily outperforming its peer group. The FTSE All Share Index hardly moved in that period. The WEIF had assets of over

£10 billion at its peak. In 2015, WIM launched a closed end fund called Woodford Patient Capital Trust (WPCT) that also became a record breaker when it raised £800 million, to invest in largely unquoted companies. In 2017 there followed a more concentrated version of Neil Woodford's best ideas, the Woodford Income Focus Fund (WIFF).

WIM had big and enthusiastic backers in the shape of St James's Place (SJP), a private wealth management company and Hargreaves Lansdown, the UK's largest investment platform, and soon the total funds under management were to swell to £15 billion as both of these influential companies cranked up their marketing efforts and included Woodford funds in their own portfolios. Importantly, both WEIF and WIFF were included in the Hargreaves Lansdown Wealth 50 list of highly recommended funds. Fund managers would be delighted to get just one fund on this influential list, let alone two.

It was all going rather well.

Hubris to humble pie

Following its launch in June 2014, after an excellent initial period the WEIF outperformed the FTSE All Share Index by 14% in the three years to June 2017. But from late 2017 many of its key bets started to turn sour. The table on the next page shows the performance of the fund's top ten holdings over the eighteen months from December 2017. There were other significant holdings that were not quite in the fund's top ten that also hit the buffers badly. These included Capita, Kier, AA, Eve Sleep, e-Therapeutics and Circassia. Woodford seemed to continuously throw good money after bad as these stocks fell hard and re-financings were required.

Performance of Woodford Equity Income Fund top 10
18 months from 31 December 2017

	Weight in fund at Dec 2017 %	Price at Dec 2017 p	Price at June 2019 p	Change %
Imperial Brands	6.9	3166	1951	−38
AstraZeneca	6.8	5121	6438	26
Legal & General	4.9	273	275	1
Lloyds	3.4	68	56	−18
Burford Capital	3.4	1152	1592	38
Barratt Developments	2.8	647	574	−11
Purplebricks	2.7	416	98	−76
Prothena	2.6	36	10	−72
Provident Finanacial	2.4	657	412	−37
IP Group	2.4	142	73	−49
FTSE All Share		4221	4056	−4

Source: Hargreaves Lansdown and Woodford Equity Income Fund Fact Sheet at 31 December 2017

Mostly big losses in WEIF top 10 holdings

His stock selection system fell apart. He quickly moved from hero to zero in the eyes of investors.

After a period of dreadful performance and redemptions from unhappy investors, the WEIF was suspended on 3 June 2019 as it was clear that because the portfolio included so many small and unquoted companies, it would be unable to liquidate these holdings sufficiently quickly to satisfy investors wanting their money back. It was the request by Kent County Council to sell its £263 million holding that was the straw that broke the back of the WEIF and in total £3.6 billion of investors' money was now frozen. Most

Dreadful performance followed by fund suspension

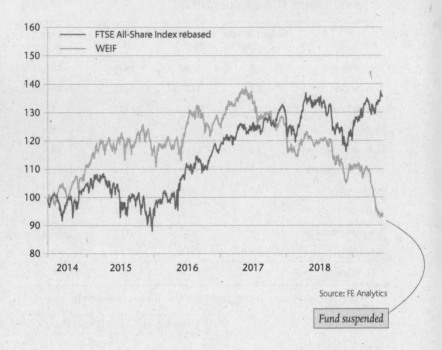

FTSE All-Share Index rebased
WEIF

Source: FE Analytics

Fund suspended

in the know had concerns well before the fund was suspended. It was no surprise to many in the City, especially amongst those fund managers who competed with the WEIF for the attention of investors' money, that the fund's exposure to illiquid investments was going to end in tears. It was a mystery to many how an experienced fund manager could countenance taking positions in such small and illiquid companies knowing that if there was just one redemption request from a large investor in the fund, it would be difficult to satisfy the demand for cash. But why was this not

Then and now: compare and contrast

Woodford Equity Income Fund as at 30 April 2019

Top 10 holdings	Mkt Cap £m	% of fund
Barratt Developments	5900	7.53
Burford Capital	3300	5.78
Taylor Wimpey	5100	5.37
Provident Finanacial	1000	4.81
Theravance Biopharma	710	4.71
Benevolent AI – unquoted	1500	4.47
IP Group	794	3.30
Countryside Properties	1300	3.13
Autolus	553	3.13
Oxford Nanopore – unquoted	1500	2.57
Ave mkt cap	**2166**	

Source: Woodford Equity Income Fund Fact Sheet April 2019

Invesco Perpetual High Income Fund as at 31 January 2014

Top 10 holdings	Mkt Cap £m	% of fund
AstraZeneca	50265	9.99
GlaxoSmithKline	78213	8.85
BT	35964	6.26
Roche	144952	5.49
BAE Systems	13861	5.48
British American Tobacco	66271	4.89
Imperial Tobacco	20894	4.81
Reckitt Benckiser	30116	4.45
Capita	10262	4.29
Rolls Royce	22440	4.09
Ave mkt cap	**47324**	

Source: Invesco Perpetual High Income Fund Fact Sheet January 2014

a worry to its main promoters at Hargreaves Lansdown? Or the financial regulator, the FCA?

The signs

Prior to the crisis, there had been a series of 'buyer beware' signals in the information provided publicly by the WEIF. They were mostly missed or ignored – perhaps because of Neil Woodford's impressive track record at Invesco Perpetual. But that was some time ago and he was now playing an entirely different game – investing in small and even unquoted companies where he had no previous form at all and where he continuously failed to read the signs from other investors that perhaps he had made a series of poor investment decisions.

A change of style

The table on the previous page shows the top ten holdings of the large Invesco Perpetual High Income Fund in 2014, the year that Neil Woodford left. The top ten is full of blue chip companies where there was a high conviction that dividends would be paid to support the income requirements of the investors in the fund. A cash flow analysis of the various companies told us that. The fund after all included the expression 'High Income' in its name and many would have expected it to do exactly what it said on the tin – in other words invest in large dividend paying companies. The average size of the companies that were included in the top ten of the Invesco Perpetual High Income Fund was £47 billion, the largest of which was the Swiss healthcare giant Roche.

In contrast the WEIF's top ten in April 2019, shortly before its suspension, included two companies that were not even listed on any exchange and the rest were significantly smaller than what investors would typically think should be included in a large income fund. The average size of companies in this new top ten was a mere £2 billion and we are being kind here as the two unquoted stocks were valued not by the market, but a small number of interested investors which arguably included connected parties. Rather like a successful sportsman who chances his arm at a different sport and fails, Neil Woodford's adventure into the world of private companies and small companies was much more likely to fail than succeed. He was just not experienced enough.

Illiquidity rises

It is very easy to get sucked into investing in smaller companies. Management are often enthusiastic and far too optimistic and it takes an experienced fund manager to see through it all and get to the nitty gritty. Smaller companies are much more likely to struggle or even crash than prove to be unicorns. You have to be a cynic to be a good smaller company investor. And once you commit to investing in a smaller company it is often some time before the opportunity to sell arises. A fund manager must at all times have an eye on a fund's liquidity. It is often the case that as a fund grows in size, the size of companies in it increases but that was not the case with the WEIF. In fact it was the opposite. The proportion of the fund, that comprised smaller companies with low liquidity and unquoted companies with no liquidity at all, remained high and actually rose as investors sold the poorly performing fund. But this was always clear from the helpful WEIF monthly factsheets. By the end of 2018, liquid investments made up just 16% of the fund. Illiquid investments made up the rest.

2018 Woodford Equity Income Fund – illiquidity rises

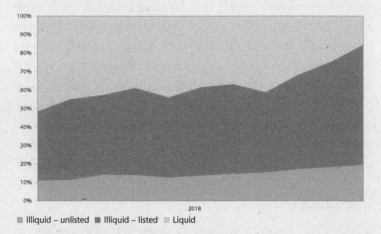

■ Illiquid – unlisted ■ Illiquid – listed ■ Liquid

Source: Bloomberg

For some time the unquoted companies in the WEIF made up 10% of the fund's assets, oddly an allowable amount as far as the financial regulator, the FCA, was concerned, and something that surely will change for funds that allow daily dealing. But really it was more like 20% before the fund got suspended because four companies – Benevolent AI, Ombu, Industrial Heat and Sabina were listed on the Guernsey Stock Exchange, a ruse that fooled no one.

Brexit uncertainty ignored

The UK political debate of the decade was seemingly ignored when investments were made for the WEIF. This was demonstrated by the fund taking large positions in housebuilders like Barratt Developments, Taylor Wimpey, Crest Nicholson and Countryside

Properties. Most asset prices usually fall in periods of uncertainty, especially property. In addition the WEIF took on large positions in other UK domestically focussed companies such as Provident Financial, Kier, NewRiver, Stobart and BCA Marketplace (which to be fair came good as it was taken over). But the positioning towards companies that did all their business in the UK domestic market was a move that was hard to justify and not surprisingly went sour due to the Brexit uncertainties.

Great minds think alike … or do they?

Curiously WEIF, WIFF and WPCT invested in many of the same companies as Invesco Perpetual. This was perhaps understandable as many people in the two investment teams had worked together in the past but the extent of the common holdings was surprising. The table on the next page shows the extent of the common holdings between these two independent fund managers at times. This is important because whilst both fund management teams were enthusiastic at the same time about a surprisingly large number of the same companies, their gusto for them could presumably change at the same time too, meaning holdings would be more difficult to unload and the high volume of selling would certainly put significant pressure on the share prices as both fund managers took concerted action once again.

Where is the income?

In April 2019, WEIF had 101 holdings and apart from some of the larger holdings, many of which were UK domestic companies enduring the uncertainties of Brexit, there was a paucity of dividend paying companies. In fact many of the companies in the

Common holdings – WIM and Invesco Perpetual

Company	WIM owns %	Invesco Perpetual owns %
4D Pharma	27	14
Allied Minds	27	19
Amigo	10	9
BCA Marketplace	7	16
Benchmark	12	16
Brave Bison	20	9
Burford Capital	9	13
Card Factory	7	27
Circassia	28	24
Crystal Amber	17	29
e-Therapeutics	17	31
Eddie Stobart Logistics	25	5
Evofem	25	20
Honeycomb Investment Trust	22	36
Horzon Discovery	13	4
Hvivo	29	26
Idex	25	16
Imperial Brands	3	2
IP Group	10	27
Mercia Technologies	25	29
Mereo Biopharma	30	20
Netscientific	47	17
NewRiver	13	26
Non Standard Finance	26	29
Oakley Capital	17	20
Provident Financial	24	22
Raven Property	13	31
Redde	20	29
Safe Harbour	26	26
Silence Therapeutics	48	12
Stobart	18	25
Thin Film Electronics	27	15
Time Out	16	12
Tissue Regenix	29	26
Xeros	40	15

Source: marketscreener.com

WEIF were the opposite of dividend paying in that they required cash from existing or new investors – as is usually the case with smaller and unquoted companies as they seek to grow. It was clear that the WEIF would need to rely on the disposal of shares in its portfolio to satisfy investors' requirement for income.

Interestingly, WEIF, Invesco Income Fund and Invesco High Income Fund were not included in the important UK Equity Income sector of funds compiled by Morningstar, perhaps because their constituent investments (i.e. companies) failed to provide an adequate level of income. Instead they were included in the much larger UK All Companies sector. This was a clear warning sign that the WEIF, as far as others were concerned, was not investing in a sufficient number of dividend paying companies to warrant inclusion in this important grouping of income funds.

Turkeys do not vote for Christmas

Unquoted company valuations played a very significant part in the performance of the WEIF. We know that from the fund's inception in June 2014 up to the beginning of 2019, when WEIF made the controversial transfer of five unquoted companies to the WPCT, the unquoted holdings represented around a staggering 40% of the fund's performance over that period.

The problem with this is who valued them? Benevolent AI (a clever company that sieves clinical data and research to find cures for diseases), Proton Partners International (a provider of a range of cancer treatments) and Industrial Heat (a cold fusion company that was supposed to create energy from small nuclear reactions) are cases in point. But there are others. Valuations of some of these companies had been dependent in the past partly or in whole by the original investors, in some cases WIM itself and that raises questions that need to be answered before one can be happy. In the same way that turkeys do not generally vote for Christmas, shareholders in unquoted companies do not generally welcome a downward adjustment to company valuations in a financing exercise if they can help it, especially if they are putting in more of their own money.

Benevolent AI

For example, at the beginning of 2015 Benevolent AI was apparently worth about £200 million but later in that year it raised just £7.6 million extra cash even though it had £48 million on its balance sheet in 2014. Why raise such a small amount of money when the balance sheet was already stuffed with it? But this time the very small financing valued the company at close to £1.2 billion. What could have caused this dramatic increase in valuation? This was a very helpful valuation uplift and was the single largest contribution to WEIF's performance in 2015 as it increased the valuation of the holding in Benevolent AI by six times. The WEIF owned 18% of unquoted Benevolent AI. WIM owned even more.

Oxford Nanopore

Another unquoted company in the WEIF portfolio was Oxford Nanopore Technologies, a company that analyses DNA sequences, the building blocks of genes. The secret to life itself. Any company that can answer that question deserves a Godlike valuation status but a financing in 2015 took the valuation of this special company from £750 million to £1.12 billion – a 50% increase. All we know is that this financing was supported by new and existing investors and that included the WEIF. Oxford Nanopore Technologies may have the potential to be a life transforming company but over £40 million of losses were reported in 2015, and there was virtually no revenue at that time.

Smaller the better for some but not for others

St James's Place (SJP), a wealth management company, was a fan of WIM. But not a big fan. If it had been, it would have let WIM invest in smaller and unquoted companies, as the WEIF did. But SJP still handed WIM a lucrative billion pound mandate to run its high income fund as long as WIM stuck to investing in larger companies. The performance of these two funds over the first eighteen months is starkly different and is shown in the chart below. The absence

WEIF versus SJP High Income Fund

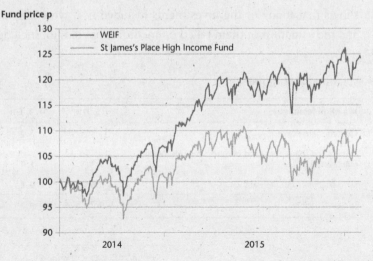

Source: Financial Express

of smaller and unquoted companies caused the SJP High Income Fund to underperform the WEIF by nearly 16% in just eighteen months from launch. Quite a lot really. The SJP High Income Fund failed to benefit from the significant uplift in valuations reported by the WEIF in small and unquoted companies over this key initial period which curiously was a period when UK smaller companies advanced by a moderate 5%. The beneficial effect that the choices of smaller and unquoted companies included in the WEIF was clear and deserved investigation.

Valuation warning signs

At all times investment managers should be aware of the liquidity of the fund they run and have in mind the ability to sell sufficient investments within a reasonable time to respond to investors' demands for their money back. This is a sound requirement for funds that deal daily. The 2015 WEIF Annual Report clearly shows that many of the investments included in it were illiquid and the valuation of them relied on methods that did not include

Valuation technique

Valuation technique	2015, £m	2014, £m
Quoted share prices	5.3	3.0
Not quoted share prices but derived from observable market data	2.3	1.0
Not observable market data	0.6	0.2
Total WEIF value	8.2	4.2

Source: 2015 WEIF Annual Report

> *Significant increase of value of fund measured by means other than quoted share prices in 2015 from 28% to 35%*

reference to quoted share prices. This is odd and as time went on the method of valuing the fund became more opaque. Of the 106 investments included in the 2015 WEIF Annual Report over half were either unquoted or AIM listed companies where the liquidity was severely restricted. All this was public information but who again was looking?

Offloading

In a very unusual swap in March 2019, the WEIF offloaded a package of stakes in five unquoted companies apparently worth £73 million to WPCT, an investment trust managed by WIM itself. They were not the sort of companies that would usually be in a high profile large income fund. The five were Atom Bank (a challenger bank), Cell Medica (a company that aimed to re-programme human immune cells to just attack cancer cells), RateSetter (a peer to peer lending company), Carrick Therapeutics (another cancer specialist) and Spin,Memory (an MRAM company that aimed to store memory using the theory of magnetism rather than electrical charges known as DRAM). In return the WEIF was issued new shares in WPCT valued at their net asset value and making up nearly 10% of the trust. As WPCT traded at a significant discount to its net asset value, WEIF paid a premium over the price at which the trust's shares traded in the market at that time. It was a surprise to many that this share swap was ever undertaken at all and also that it was done by issuing shares in WPCT at its estimated net asset value rather than the price that the market gave to the shares.

It gets worse for the WEIF. In addition to paying a premium for the WPCT shares, the WEIF agreed to pay a further £6 million to the trust for undertakings already given to some of the five companies for future funding. On the day the new WPCT shares were issued to the WEIF they were worth £68 million. So all in all WEIF investors probably lost out by about £10 million or so on day one of this transaction. As WPCT's share price continued to fall that loss just got bigger.

But we now know why it was necessary to offload so many unquoted companies in exchange for shares in WPCT, a listed investment trust. The WEIF was experiencing big redemptions from investors because of its poor performance and worries about its smaller company exposure generally. It had already sold stakes in the more liquid larger companies in the portfolio but because many of these had performed so badly, the unquoted company proportion of the fund's assets was rising and looked like it was going to breach the FCA's limit of 10%. Desperate measures were required. In truth the WEIF was already over this 10% limit as a number of its unquoted companies were excluded from this constraint as they had announced that they were going to float within a year. What a stupid dispensation allowed by the regulator whose job it was to protect investors.

Lesson

You back a fund manager because he continues to do what he has proved he can do well. When a fund manager adopts a completely different untried and untested strategy you are entitled to pause for breath and say 'not with my money'. Neil Woodford's move from investing in large dividend paying companies when he was under supervison at Invesco Perpetual, to smaller companies and unquoted biotech companies at WIM, where he ran the money and owned the company, was just such a move to be wary of.

In addition an analysis of the WEIF would have indicated there was almost a wanton disregard for the requirements of daily trading in the fund.

As the WEIF headed towards its inevitable 'gating' a number of ruses were employed to satisfy the weak FCA rules designed to protect investors, but these were just more warning signs that the fund was in trouble. Because of the suspension of the WEIF due to its failure to ensure appropriate liquidity, there will inevitably be more regulation in this area for active fund managers in the UK. This may well mean smaller companies will find it tougher to get finance from equity markets, hitherto an important source of money for exciting and growing companies, and one where the UK stock market up to now has excelled. The full cost of the Woodford debacle is yet to be counted.

Conclusion

DIVING LESSONS

When the high cliff divers of Acapulco are perched on the towering rocks at La Quebrada in Mexico we all know what happens next. They plummet in a precipitous dive at 55mph with fists clenched to protect themselves from the swelling sea below. They sometimes get injured but there has never been a fatality. However, for companies that suffer share price dives that resemble the plunges made by the high cliff divers of Acapulco, the consequences for investors almost always involve long-term financial pain and in the worst cases, when companies go bust, they lose their entire investment.

Many of the share price dives that feature in this book – some of which resulted in the companies concerned disappearing altogether and all of which resulted in considerable harm to investors and other stakeholders – were as steep as the divers' plunges, though some were more drawn-out swallow dives.

Like the inevitable plunges of the high cliff divers of Acapulco as they spread their arms wide and say their prayers before they commence their dive, all the price falls in this book were foreseeable. From an inspection of the reported numbers it was clear that future expectations were not going to be met or previous results and performances were not as good as they appeared at first sight. It was only a matter of time before the share prices dived or in the case of the Woodford Equity Income Fund (WEIF), the fund's unit price collapsed.

The signs were there

Although a company's annual report focuses on the past, it provides a guide to the future – and while things may look fine and dandy on the surface, for those who take the trouble to look, an annual report or a fund manager's monthly report may well contain clues that all is not quite as it seems. That was the case with all the companies in this book and the WEIF: the signs were there that they were all heading for a fall because that's what the numbers told us. In fact, sometimes it was only one number. And dive they did, most in a way that the great Raoul Garcia, one of the best known and most well respected of the high cliff divers of Acapulco, would have been proud of.

The ten warning signs highlighted in the annual reports of the companies in this book are a representative rather than an exhaustive list of common indicators that things were going to get worse before they got better. The diving lessons are that a significant and possibly disastrous share price fall is likely when a company's annual report shows it has:

■ A deteriorating current asset quality, where there is an increase in the subjectivity in valuing them. Amounts recoverable on contracts which may take ages to collect are lower quality current assets when compared with cash or invoiced receivables that should be collected quickly.

- Large and increasing accruals of revenue where chosen accounting policies allow the recognition of revenue far ahead of the cash actually being received.

- Large and seemingly unsubstantiated goodwill amounts on its balance sheet, where the assumptions used for forecasting future cash flows from previously acquired businesses bear no resemblance whatsoever to the present trading conditions.

- Been relying on acquisitions to keep profits moving ahead. Acquisitions can allow short-term profits to be manipulated through the use of provisions and so-called reorganisation costs that are accounted for away from the headline profits of the company.

- Disclosed related party transactions. Run a mile from any company that does business with related parties. No ifs and buts. Just run.

- Reported worrying trends in its performance. A deteriorating set of numbers over time showing rising stock levels, poor cash flow, falling margins or big increases in working capital can be a trend that is your friend, telling you to avoid the shares.

- Growing levels of stock or makes odd adjustments to its stock valuation. Growing levels of stock may mean there is likely to be an obsolescence problem in the future, with the shock of lower profits being reported.

- Capitalised large costs that under normal circumstances would be expected to pass through the income statement. Capitalising costs allows higher profits to be reported until, of course, the costs that were capitalised are written off and lower profits are finally reported some time later.

- Auditors who may be conflicted, as they also bill substantial amounts for non-audit services. There are rules on this these days, but they are not that strict and whatever the auditors may say about there being no conflict, they must find it hard to be totally independent and objective.

- Been too optimistic as to the recoverability of its debts and failed to provide adequately for bad ones. Banks have been guilty of this in the past but thankfully disclosure in annual reports is better now and it should be easy enough to see if bad debt provisions are not keeping up with the growth in the business.

In the case of the WEIF, there were many worrying signals but the fact that the strategy of the fund was wholly different to the one that made Neil Woodford's reputation at Invesco Perpetual was surely enough of a warning sign.

The system wasn't working

In some of the cases in this book the auditors have been censured by the auditors' regulator, the Financial Reporting Council (FRC). But this has always been after the damage has been done, whereas the signs were there well before the companies' share prices plunged. The annual reports told us all we needed to know. But who was looking? Not the FRC it seems.

It's fashionable these days to blame the auditors when companies go bust or share prices take a tumble, and in many of the cases in this book they can justifiably take the rap for not doing a proper job. But there are others in the frame, too, who have taken less of a rap. Institutional investors, for instance, are increasingly sophisticated these days and could do more to ensure the soundness of the business in which they are investing – including choosing the auditor and perhaps even the audit partner after a selection process. Heaven knows corporate governance and risk departments have mushroomed at investment management companies recently and they could be put to better use by having a say in who audits their investments. Bankers and advisors get privileged access to companies' information but then remain silent if it suits.

Audit committees not only need to up their game but they should include fewer of the same old faces from the non-executive merry-go-round. And then there are the regulators who seem, well … not to act until it's too late. They have been reactive in the past and need to be more proactive. This applies to both the FRC and the FCA.

Auditors, regulators, bankers, advisors and investors – they all have a role to play in the way the system operates for stock market listed companies. Influential wealth management and fund and share dealing platforms such as Hargreaves Lansdown need in particular to ensure that their due diligence processes identify flaws in funds before recommending them – or persisting to recommend them. The fortunes of those who invest through these platforms depend on them doing so.

Pressure on management

The pressure is on for the management of listed companies and indeed fund managers to perform. Share prices are valued more on expectations and not the past, so hitting the forecasts and even exceeding them is the way share prices go up. If they fail to meet expectations and the share price suffers they may well lose their jobs and investors will find someone else to move the company on and the share price up. The pressure is on for management to do everything in their grasp to make sure that the expectations are met, and that usually means profits need to rise over time and the balance sheet's quality needs to be maintained or better still enhanced by a growing cash balance, or at least a reduction in debt.

This is where our flexible friends – the accounting standards – come in. They provide guidance as to how accounting transactions are recorded and reported but they are not proscriptive and judgements and estimates often need to be made in their application. This is the problem and it leaves them open to abuse as the temptation to keep profits moving up (or at least not down) is high. Management can stretch the rules and sometimes they cross the line that divides honest delusion from criminal fraud.

For funds investing in illiquid assets that do not trade daily on an exchange, there must be far stricter controls to ensure that liquidity measures are appropriate and that investors will be able to cash in their investments when they need to. The 'gating' of the WEIF was no different to what happened in the case of several large property funds back in 2008, so there were precedents.

Unquoted company valuations are often too spurious to include in portfolio valuations that are used to price funds available to retail investors. It is fine in closed-end investment trusts to use unquoted company valuations to calculate a value of a portfolio, as the uncertainty is reflected in the discount of the fund's price to its net asset value which is derived from a large number of buyer and sellers having an input. But with open-ended unit trusts that are priced by those who administer them there is an additional level of subjectivity that is open to abuse that really ought not to be there. Rather like the flexibility that accounting standards can offer companies when recording certain transactions, examples of which are identified in this book, the valuation of unquoted companies for inclusion in daily traded investment funds offers the same elasticity to ensure targets can be met.

Watchdog not bloodhound: the auditor's role

An audit is an independent examination of the financial statements of a company. The auditor is required to form an opinion as to whether the financial statements show a true and fair view of its financial position and whether they have been prepared in line with the relevant accounting standards and company law. Auditors should do the appropriate amount and type of work to test the numbers presented by the directors of the company in order to identify any material mis-statements. They should also ensure that the financial statements include disclosures required by accounting standards and company law. The audit will involve the auditors asking management questions as to how they have been arrived at and to justify any large numbers included in the accounts. The auditors' requirements also extend to securing written acknowledgements (that is, proof or warranties) of things like debts owed to the company.

The key characteristics of an audit are therefore that: it is an *independent examination* where the auditor *forms an opinion* on the financial statements; it entails undertaking *adequate work* to identify any material mis-statements; there are *required disclosures* in the financial statements; and the auditor will have *made enquiries* with management. Where an audit fails, it is often because *adequate work* was not carried out.

The audit does not pass comment on the directors of the company or the company strategy; it does not test all the internal controls; it does not check all the numbers in the financial statements; and it does not check all the transactions in a given period. Importantly, an audit is not designed to check for fraud, as some people think. In short, auditors are watchdogs, not bloodhounds.

Big four, big problem

The international accounting world is dominated by just four giant accounting firms – KPMG, EY, PwC and Deloitte. Some time ago there used to be the Big Eight, but the regulators made the mistake of allowing them to merge into the Big Four, leaving less competition. Some would say that there is virtually no competition as companies will rarely appoint auditors who audit or supply non-audit services to their competitors. There is not a Big Four in international law firms or other professions, so why in auditing? A way needs to be found to help other firms to grow and provide more competition in the auditing of large listed companies and recent recommendations should help this process.

Because of many of the accounting and auditing scandals included in this book and others like BHS, there has been a cry for change. The UK Department of Business, Energy and Industrial Strategy Select Committee's Future of Audit enquiry has proposed that the Big Four should be broken up which would separate their auditing and highly profitable consultancy arms and reduce the potential for conflicts of interest. The Big Four audit nearly all the UK's top 100 companies and some have suggested that these should be undertaken with the help of some of the smaller audit firms. This they say would provide a check on the audit work, which is a good idea, though whether the smaller audit firms are up to the challenge is another matter. It is also argued that there should be a limit to the market share of the Big Four auditors of the companies included in the FTSE 100.

I believe that auditors should not be broken up into audit firms and consultancies. Audit costs may rise as a result. Also, young trainee auditors should have the opportunity to do more rewarding consultancy work. Generally, young auditors are smart people and if they are excluded from doing non-audit work, the talent pool for the important but sometimes dull audit work lessens – and that is bad news for audits generally. Young accountants, like any trainee professional, need to do the hard yards before entering the sunlit uplands of their chosen profession. But increasingly auditing is being done by over-worked young graduates and therefore is being pushed down the skills ladder just as the expectations (and criticisms) of auditors are rising.

It is time for audit committees to step up to the plate – and perhaps auditors should be mandated to be on them. That way they would gain a better insight into the broader activities of the company and also into potentially contentious issues involving accounting throughout the year rather than just at the year end. Forewarned is forearmed. They should be forced to investigate signs that indicate concerns around a company. For example they need to address why hedge funds are short of its shares or why the shares are valued at a lower level than a competitor's. They need to address in public any potential corporate governance concerns and perhaps dramatic changes in company strategy and accounting policies – all of which are common signs that a company is troubled and may be in danger of failing. They should also remember that many of the warning signs that a company is heading for a fall have been seen before time and time again. History repeats itself.

Following the Competition and Markets Authority's (CMA) Final Report into statutory audit, which concurred with much of what has been said above, an Independent Review into the Quality and Effectiveness of the UK Audit Market was set up under Sir Donald Brydon and was expected to report by the end of 2019.

But the lessons for auditors from the share price plunges recounted in this book are many. Auditor rotation is a good thing, as over time directors and auditors risk becoming too familiar with each other; indeed, too reliant on each other. Companies are obliged to put their audit out to tender every ten years and they should change their auditors every twenty years. This is far too long for large companies in the UK and it encourages the relationship to be less than independent.

The provincial offices of the Big Four seem to have had more than their fair share of mishaps. My suspicion is that they may sometimes have become over reliant on a handful of clients. For a provincial office of a Big Four firm to lose a FTSE 350 company as an audit client because of disagreements would have a larger effect on the practice than had it been lost by head office in London. A large portion of the companies included in this book were audited by the provincial offices of the Big Four firms.

In some circumstances, the auditor may be hopelessly ill equipped to audit certain balances. For example, work in progress – in particular, partially completed construction contracts – are very difficult items to audit. In cases like these, an auditor may have no choice but to rely on directors' assurances as to the degree of completion of contracts and the costs required to complete them. Perhaps it is better to call in experts in construction projects, for example, to verify the directors' assurances. We know from Carillion and others that reported profits for construction companies are particularly dependent on valuing amounts recoverable on contracts. In Carillion's case, it was the value of large, partially completed hospitals that the auditors – perhaps unsurprisingly – failed to get their heads round.

Conflicts of interest can be a problem where an audit firm also supplies a company with lucrative services, such as consultancy. To maintain its independence, surely an audit company should refrain from proffering other services to a company while it is its auditor? For example, Autonomy's auditors charged £1.2 million for non-audit services and £1.5 million for audit fees in 2010, the year before Hewlett-Packard made its disastrous takeover of the company. How much did the money being earned for non-audit work influence the rigour with which the audit was carried out? Who knows? But the potential for conflict is clear and should be avoided – a view no doubt held by Hewlett-Packard.

A cosy club

The Financial Reporting Council (FRC) is for the moment the main regulator of companies' accounts, auditors and accountants in the UK. The FRC's aim is to promote high-quality corporate governance and reporting and, by doing this, show the world that the UK is a good place to invest and do business. It also holds those blamed for wrongdoing to account. Its work is meant to be a key component in ensuring both the vibrancy and trustworthiness of UK capital markets. It is full of committees but, unhelpfully for the regulator of accountants, these were full of accountants often from the Big Four. Some might suggest that the FRC resembled a cosy private club for old chums with a lot in common. But following the Kingman Review into the FRC, things are changing.

The trouble with the FRC was that, rather like the Keystone Cops, who always arrived late to the scene of a crime, their important investigations often commenced sometime after the damage had been done.

In the past the FRC had been a rather obscure regulator which no one really paid much attention to until the fallout from some really quite large company failures – Carillion in particular – threw the spotlight on its role and performance.

My view is that it is rare indeed that there are no warning signs ahead of a company failure (this book is full of them) and auditors must be aware of these as they go about their work. It therefore follows that the FRC should be making sure that auditors are aware of them and drawing their attention to them.

Kingman took the view that the FRC was from an altogether different era and had not moved with the times. He said it was not fit for purpose perhaps because of its closeness to those it regulated – mainly the Big Four. He said that it should be abolished and a new body, the Audit, Reporting and Governance Authority (ARGA) should be set up, funded by the state (unlike the levy on audit firms the FRC had been reliant on and which he felt risked it being unwilling to bite the hand that fed it) and that its management should be recruited from those less connected to those it regulates. The review also concluded that there should be more attention given to potential warning signs that there may be trouble ahead and that auditors should have a duty to alert investors to any concerns they have. And in order to ensure that investigations were carried out in a timely fashion – they certainly are not at present – it was recommended that

ARGA should be able to appoint appropriately skilled people to carry out reviews.

For some auditors all this change and the potential for reputational damage, fines, loss of livelihood and general stress may prove too much. We have seen that the accountants Grant Thornton no longer wish to be appointed auditors to Sports Direct and it should surprise no one that they will not be the last who quit. If there is a hint of scandal about a company then it may in future be more difficult to find an auditor to sign off accounts.

A shortage of good independent research

Access to quoted companies for investors used to be fairly easy, as long as they were not in a close season when they were likely to be in possession of price-sensitive information. Just pick up the phone and the company would be there. Fund managers often say that what has most influence over their investment decisions is meeting company management. But company managers are less available for meetings these days and the presentations they make, while being more formalised and slicker, tend not to be terribly informative. Management stick to the script and rarely stray. It is now more difficult to get to the nuggety bits of how a company works.

Also, the volume of research produced by investment analysts has fallen as, to be frank, has its quality – the result of lower commissions on share dealing, lower volumes of shares traded, research now having to be paid for by fund managers out of their own pocket and fewer good people producing it. It is sad to say that no one ever got really rich from writing incisive, deep and investigative research alone. The reduction in quality and volume of independent research has quickened as a result of the EU Markets in Financial Instruments Directive (MIFLD II), which regulates firms who provide services to clients linked to financial instruments (shares, bonds, units in collective investment schemes and derivatives), and which is seen by many as a disaster. There will be even less research available in the future. Some of the best investment analysts are moving fast to the buy side or are being completely lost by the industry. Admittedly some of the research was pretty dreadful, but this was often ignored by the market anyway – and losing voices, any voices, in a market is a problem. Research appeared to be free to fund managers, as they would pay for it indirectly through commissions on share dealing. Not any more.

A lot is changing, which means that the investor is less likely to be well informed, there will be less debate about companies and fewer decision makers and influencers. The market in information is the same as any other market – the more players the better. MIFLD II just reduced the number of players. This will result in an even lower volume of shares traded, which will mean more volatility, especially in small and mid-sized companies – probably not what the architect of MIFLD II intended. So, the annual report will become an even more important document that will be relied upon even more by investors in order to understand the companies they are investing in. The pressure is on to ensure that the annual report is an even more effective, helpful and reliable document. More investors will need to read these important documents themselves in future and know what to look for and where to find it – this was often a job done by the much-maligned research analysts. But they are not there so much these days. That is why I hope that the examples in this book will help investors to cut through the gloss and propaganda of the first sections of any public company's annual report and get to the nitty-gritty, nuggety bits in the numbers towards the end of the document. One unexplained outlier of a number is often all it takes to tell you that the shares are ones to avoid. This is the Iceberg Principle.

Many market participants – auditors, regulators, institutional investors, bankers, accountants, and company management have rightly taken flack for some of the recent share price disasters that have cost investors billions. But in all the examples in this book, the signs were there in the important annual report that a share price dive was imminent – it was only a matter of when not if.

Fortunately, many of the thoughts, observations and proposals in the first edition of this book seem to have been taken on board by the various enquiries that have followed the recent string of audit failures and company disasters, and have been incorporated into their recommendations. If these recommendations are now adopted by government, this should make it easier for investors to avoid the kinds of losses this book is all about. But even so, investors will always need to keep an eye out for the red flags and signs that there may be trouble ahead. History has a habit of repeating itself.

Glossary

Here are brief explanations of some of the terms and abbreviations in this book.

Accounting policies The principles, procedures and rules consistently applied by a company to prepare its financial statements. Accounting policies must be disclosed in the annual report and these will include the way depreciation rates, goodwill and stock valuations are calculated.

Accounting standards Companies that have their shares traded on a regulated public market must prepare their accounts in accordance with International Financial Reporting Standards (IFRS). These are issued by the International Accounting Standards Board (IASB). IFRS are slowly replacing many different national accounting standards and are designed to ensure accounts are comparable and can be understood around the globe. Accounting standards that were issued by the predecessor of the IASB, the International Accounting Standards Committee (IASC), are called International Accounting Standards (IAS) and are still used today as they have not all been replaced by IFRS. Details of particular accounting standards that feature in this book are given at the end of this glossary.

Accruals Costs incurred by a company but for which the supplier has not yet issued an invoice. They are often estimates of what is owed.

Accrued income Income that a company says it has earned but it has not yet invoiced the customer for and neither has it received the cash. Accrued income is recognised in the period that it has been earned and not in the period when the cash is received.

AIM The Alternative Investment Market, a more lightly regulated market in the UK that allows smaller less established companies to float and raise finance.

Amortisation The way an intangible asset, such as development costs that have been capitalised in the balance sheet, are expensed through the income statement over a number of years – the reduction of the asset's value on the balance sheet each year being equivalent to the amortisation cost recorded in the income statement. Amortisation starts as soon as the asset is available for use and the period over which the amortisation takes place should reflect either the way the asset is consumed (which may vary from year to year) or the expected useful life of the asset (in which case the same amount is amortised for each year of that expected useful life in what is called straight line depreciation).

ARGA Audit, Reporting and Governance Authority. Following the collapse of Carillion, a review into how the FRC functioned was conducted in 2018 by Sir John Kingman, who recommended that a new regulatory body, accountable to Parliament, be established to replace the FRC. The aim of ARGA is to provide a more effective oversight into the audit profession and to address its concentration in particular. The Big 4 auditors currently audit 98% of the companies in the FTSE 350.

Audit The independent examination of the financial statements of a company. All companies are required by law to be independently audited by a recognised auditor. The auditor needs to form an opinion as to whether the numbers that are presented show a true and fair view of the company's financial position and are in line with relevant accounting standards and company law. The audit also needs to ensure that the required disclosures are made in the financial statements.

Audit committees Listed companies in the US and UK must have an audit committee and it should include at least two independent non-executive directors. The audit committee must monitor the integrity of the financial statements, check internal controls and the effectiveness of internal audit, oversee the appointment of the internal auditor and develop a non-audit services policy for the existing auditor.

Balance sheet Sometimes called a statement of financial position, it is a list of all the assets owned and all the liabilities owed by a company at a certain date. It is a snapshot of a company's financial position. It also shows the owners' interest in the company and this is called equity. A balance sheet must always balance because the amount a company owes is equal to the amount it owns.

Banking covenants The conditions imposed on a company by its bankers when they lend money. The aim is to ensure that the company is able to pay the interest on the loan and make the required capital repayments. If a company breaks the covenants, there can be serious consequences – the loan may need to be refinanced and if this is not done, the company may go bust.

Big Four The four largest accounting firms in the world – EY,

PwC, KPMG and Deloitte. Their dominant position in audit and to some extent non-audit services is controversial. Previously, in the 1980s, before some mergers took place, there was a Big Eight consisting of Arthur Andersen, Arthur Young, Price Waterhouse, Coopers & Lybrand, Deloitte Haskins & Sells, Touche Ross, Ernst & Whinney and Peat Marwick Mitchell.

Capitalise An item is capitalised if it is recorded as an asset in the balance sheet rather than expensed through the income statement. Items of expenditure may be capitalised if they are expected to have a useful life of over one year.

Carrying value The value an asset is recorded at in the balance sheet.

Cash Money in the bank and owned by the company.

Cash flow The cash generated by a company in a given period. It is the operating profit adjusted for non-cash items like depreciation and the investment made in working capital such as inventory, creditors and debtors.

Cash generating unit (CGU) An identifiable group of assets that by themselves generate cash flows that are separate from the cash flows generated by other groups of assets. CGUs, to which goodwill has been allocated, must be tested annually to ensure that the recoverable amount is higher than its carrying value.

Cost See Expense

Creditors Those to whom a company owes money.

Current assets Assets that are expected to be converted into cash within one year. Examples include debtors and inventories.

Debtors Those who owe money to a company.

Depreciation The systematic allocation through the income statement of the cost of a fixed asset less its residual value over its estimated useful life. Tangible assets are generally depreciated while intangible assets are amortised.

Dividend Money paid by a company to its shareholders and expressed in pence or cents per share.

Dividend cover A ratio that shows by how much the dividend is covered by the company's earnings. It is a measure of how secure the dividend is. A cover of less than one indicates that the dividend is being partially paid out of retained earnings and this may not be sustainable.

Due diligence The work required to be done before a contract is signed, perhaps for the purchase of one company by another. The work will aim to provide sufficient information for an informed decision to be made about the quality of the business being acquired and indeed how much it may be worth.

EBITDA The net earnings of a company but with interest on debt, tax, depreciation and amortisation added back. The EBITDA calculation allows one company to be compared to another as it strips out the cost of debt, tax, depreciation and amortisation. These are often items that are very specific to particular companies and in some cases can be subjective in nature. EBITDA approximates closely to cash flow but importantly does not account for cash that may be absorbed by working capital.

Expense and expensed An expense, or cost, decreases economic benefits over a period of time through an outflow of cash or a reduction in assets or an increase in liabilities. An expense is said to be expensed when it passes through the income statement and is a deduction from sales. In some cases, expenses can be capitalised and recorded as assets and then depreciated through the income statement over time.

Fair value The amount an asset could be exchanged for in an arm's length transaction between willing, well-informed and knowledgeable parties.

FCA The Financial Conduct Authority. The FCA regulates companies and markets in the UK financial industry and aims to protect the consumer.

Fixed asset A tangible piece of property, such as a machine, that has a useful life of more than one year and is used by a company in its operations. A fixed asset is usually depreciated over its expected useful life and this is charged through the income statement as an addition to costs and therefore it reduces profits. There are different rules for buildings and land.

FRC The Financial Reporting Council, which regulates accountants, auditors and actuaries in the UK. Its role is to protect investors who rely on company annual reports and hold those to account who fail to keep to acceptable professional standards. Following the 2018 Kingman review, the FRC is to be replaced by ARGA.

FTSE 100 A market capitalisation index made up of the largest 100 companies listed on the London Stock Exchange (LSE). In general, the FTSE 100 index is made up of UK based companies that do their business all over the world.

FTSE 250 A market capitalisation index made up of the 101st to the 350th largest companies listed on the LSE. In general, the FTSE 250 index is made up of UK based companies that do their business in the UK.

FTSE 350 This is made up of the companies in both the FTSE 100 and FTSE 250, and so represents the 350 largest companies listed on the LSE.

Goodwill An intangible asset created when a company buys another company. It represents the difference between what was paid for that company and the fair value of the net assets acquired. It will include the value of a company's brand names, customer relationships, their own technology and patents. Each year its value has to be audited to ensure that it is not impaired.

Impairment of assets An asset is impaired if its recoverable amount is less than its carrying value.

Income statement An indicator of a company's performance over a period of time which is usually one year. Briefly, it includes the revenues and costs for a period to arrive at a profit or loss. It is also referred to as the statement of comprehensive income or the profit and loss account.

Independent research Research done by investment analysts at firms that have no connection with the company they are researching. This valuable service supplied to institutional clients by banks and brokers used to be included in the fees they charged, but since the introduction of MiFID II it now has to be charged for separately, which many think will result in less research being carried out, especially on smaller companies.

Initial public offering (IPO) The first time a company issues shares to members of the public, including institutional investors. Following an IPO, the company becomes a public company. Prior to the IPO, the company would have been a private company with perhaps a limited number of shareholders who may have included the founders of the company, their friends and family and venture capitalists.

Institutional investors Those such as asset managers, insurance companies, banks, pension funds and investment trusts who invest on others' behalf. They are deemed to be professional and the trading of the vast majority of shares on recognised exchanges is done by institutional investors.

Intangible assets Assets that are not physical and have a life of over one year. Examples include the goodwill acquired when a business is bought, patents and development expenditure.

LSE The London Stock Exchange. The main UK stock exchange on which many international and domestic companies are listed.

Market capitalisation The monetary value given to a company by investors. It is the product of multiplying the company's share price by the number of shares in issue.

MiFID II The Markets in Financial Instruments Directive II, whose issue in January 2018 affected share, bond, derivative and commodity markets and those that work in them. Its aim is to protect investors and to ensure that markets work in a fair and transparent way. One of its main effects is to ensure that asset managers pay separately for investment research. This used to be included in the commissions paid on dealing in shares. Many think that MiFID II will reduce the amount of research carried out on small and mid-sized companies and therefore is likely to have a detrimental effect on a company's ability to raise finance and the liquidity of its shares.

Mobilisation costs The costs incurred, often by a contractor, in order to set up for a long term contract. These costs may include transportation, equipment and staff costs. IAS 11 allowed for these to be capitalised and amortised over the life of the contract, but many companies expensed these costs. IFRS 15 requires these costs to be capitalised but only if certain criteria are met. The trouble with mobilisation costs is that some companies overstated them, which kept profits up.

Percentage of completion method   IAS 11 – Construction contracts, an accounting standard that used to allow revenues to be recognised in the income statement based on the proportion of the contract that was completed. Key though was the reliance on estimates, often by management, and they were sometimes wrong. IFRS 15 has superseded IAS 11 and there are now stricter rules governing revenue recognition.

PFI   Public finance initiative, a method whereby companies build and often manage public projects. A PFI enables government to avoid paying the capital cost of a project but they are then tied into a long term service contract to pay for the use of the newly built asset, such as a hospital. Some critics would say that governments use PFIs to keep debt off their balance sheets.

Present value   Today's value of a future stream of cash flows. So if interest rates are at 10% the present value of £1.10 in a year's time is £1.

Price-earnings ratio   The value of a company's shares measured in terms of the number of years of earnings that would be required to reach the current value of the shares. It is calculated by dividing the share price by the earnings per share.

Price sensitive information   Unpublished information relating to a company or its shares that is not generally available to the public but which on becoming available is likely to have an effect on the price of the shares.

Prospectus The document produced when a company wishes to issue shares and have them listed on an exchange. It is meant to contain all the material information about the company so that investors can make a well informed decision as to whether to invest or not. It will contain financial statements, a description of activities, details about the directors, significant contracts and other information. It is a detailed document and will often say more about a company than even an annual report.

Realisable value The cash that could be obtained by selling an asset in an orderly market.

Recoverable amount The higher of an asset's fair value (on the open market say) and its value in use (which can be the present value of its expected life after tax cash flows discounted at the company's cost of capital). The value in use number is often appropriate to use when there is no open market for the asset.

Related party transaction A transaction between two parties that prior to the transaction had an existing relationship. There are strict rules about these types of transactions and their details need to be disclosed in annual reports.

Reorganisation costs Costs incurred in reorganising a company's activities, perhaps the closure of a business. They are often separately identified in an income statement.

Revenue recognition The method by which companies recognise revenue in their income statement. Recently IFRS 15 has been adopted in the UK which sets strict criteria as to how and when revenue can be recognised in a company's income statement. Previously IAS 11 and IAS 18 had been used but in some cases these accounting standards were abused. IFRS 15 is a welcome new accounting standard.

Rights issue The grant of the right to buy new shares at a discounted price to existing holders in proportion to their existing holdings. There is no obligation on the shareholders to exercise their right to buy the shares and in fact they can sell their rights. Rights issues occur when companies need to raise money.

SEC The Securities and Exchange Commission, which regulates the US securities markets. Its job is to protect investors, allow capital to be raised and to promote fair, efficient and orderly markets.

Shorted When a proportion of a company's shares have been lent to hedge funds, which then sell them in the anticipation that, by the time they have to give the shares back, they will have been able to buy them back for less and therefore make a profit. If, however, the share price rises and they have to pay more to buy the shares back, they will make a loss.

Stakeholders All those who have an interest in a business and are affected by its activities. Stakeholders include employees, owners, managers, suppliers, customers, lenders, government and communities.

Trade receivables What is owed to the company for services rendered or goods sold.

Trading Statement A statement that updates the market as to how a company is trading. These are typically issued just after key trading periods that end at the half year or year end. Trading statements are also issued when trading at a company is materially worse or better than the market expects.

US GAAP The Generally Accepted Accounting Principles used in the US and published by the Financial Accounting Standards Board

(FASB). In some cases, they differ considerably from International Financial Reporting Standards (IFRS) which are published by the International Accounting Standards Board (IASB).

Working capital The sum of receivables, inventory and cash less payables. It represents the amount of capital that can be turned into cash within one year. Working capital is required to oil the wheels of business but it must not get too large otherwise cash will decline and debt will go up. A balance is therefore required between the level of working capital and cash and debt.

Some key accounting standards

IAS 2 – Inventories The accounting standard that governs the valuation of inventories. It says that inventories should be valued at the lower of cost and net realisable value.

IAS 11 – Construction contracts The old accounting standard that prescribed the way revenues and costs should be accounted for on construction contracts where work is performed over two or more accounting periods. It says that revenues and costs should be recognised by reference to the percentage of completion of the contract as long as the outcome can be estimated reliably. IAS 11 has been superseded by IFRS 15.

IAS 18 – Revenue The old accounting standard that prescribed the way that revenue from the sale of goods or the rendering of services was accounted for. It said that revenue should be recognised when it was probable that future economic benefit will flow to the entity. IAS 18 has been superseded by IFRS 15.

IAS 36 – Impairment of assets This accounting standard sets out that assets are not carried in the balance sheet at more than their recoverable amount – this is the higher of its fair value and its value in use. These assets include goodwill arising on the acquisition of a business where an annual impairment test needs to be carried out.

IAS 38 – Intangible assets An accounting standard that sets out the conditions for measuring and recognising intangible assets such as software, trademarks, development expenditure and patents. A company is required to record an intangible as an asset in its accounts if it is probable that future economic benefits will flow from it and its cost can be measured reliably. The intangible asset needs to be amortised through the income statement and must be subject to impairment testing.

IFRS 3 – Business combinations The accounting rules for when one business acquires another. It says how the assets and liabilities of the acquired company are to be recorded and disclosed and how the goodwill on acquisition is to be calculated. In simple terms the goodwill on acquisition is the difference between the purchase consideration and the fair value of the net assets acquired.

Index